UNIVERSITY CASEBOOK SERIES®

2019 SUPPLEMENT TO
FEDERAL COURTS AND THE LAW OF FEDERAL-STATE RELATIONS

NINTH EDITION

PETER W. LOW
Hardy Cross Dillard Professor of Law Emeritus
University of Virginia

JOHN C. JEFFRIES, JR.
David and Mary Harrison Distinguished Professor of Law
University of Virginia

CURTIS A. BRADLEY
William Van Alstyne Professor of Law
Duke University

The publisher is not engaged in rendering legal or other professional advice, and this publication is not a substitute for the advice of an attorney. If you require legal or other expert advice, you should seek the services of a competent attorney or other professional.

University Casebook Series is a trademark registered in the U.S. Patent and Trademark Office.

© 2019 LEG, Inc. d/b/a West Academic
    444 Cedar Street, Suite 700
    St. Paul, MN 55101
    1-877-888-1330

Printed in the United States of America

ISBN: 978-1-64242-947-3

PREFACE

This Supplement brings the 9th edition up to date through the end of the Supreme Court's Term in the summer of 2019. There are three new main cases. All were decided five-to-four, all reflect a straight liberal-conservative split, and all resolved questions of long-standing uncertainty.

***Jesner v. Arab Bank* (2018)** is the Court's latest pronouncement on the Alien Tort Statute. It replaces *Kiobel v. Royal Dutch Petroleum* (2013), which was a main case in the 9th edition. In *Kiobel*, the Supreme Court construed the Alien Tort Statute in light of the presumption against extraterritoriality and found that it did not reach certain actions by corporations in Nigeria having no direct connection with the United States. The Second Circuit had reached the same conclusion but on different grounds. That court had ruled that the Alien Tort Statute did not provide for suits against corporate defendants, 621 F.3d 111 (2d Cir. 2010), a conclusion that was obviated but not overruled by the Supreme Court's reliance on extraterritoriality. In *Jesner*, the Supreme Court accepted much of the Second Circuit's reasoning in *Kiobel* and held that the Alien Tort Statute has no application to foreign corporations.

***Rucho v. Common Cause* (2019)** is a new main case on the political question doctrine. After backing and filling for years on whether political gerrymandering could be attacked in federal court, the Supreme Court ruled that such claims are non-justiciable, primarily for the lack of "judicially manageable standards" for determining how much political influence on redistricting is too much. Justice Kagan authored a passionate dissent. The 9th edition already has two main cases on the political question doctrine, *Nixon v. United States* (1993) and *Zivotofsky v. Clinton* (2012). Both deal with important contexts, impeachment in *Nixon* and foreign affairs in *Zivotofsky*. It may be that having three main cases on this doctrine will prove unsustainable in the long run, but for now we thought it best to provide an opportunity to study the most recent case, especially given its impact on upcoming elections. Each case is interesting, and there is very little overlap.

Finally, ***Franchise Tax Board v. Hyatt* (2019)** overruled Nevada v. Hall, 440 U.S. 410 (1979). The Court held that state immunity against private suits in the courts of other states was "preserved in the constitutional design." This year's decision in *Franchise Tax Bd* was the third time that litigation reached the Supreme Court. In 2003, the Court upheld a civil suit against California in a Nevada state court on the authority of *Nevada v. Hall*. In 2016, after the death of Justice Scalia, the case returned to the Supreme Court, which split four-four on whether *Hall* should be overruled. The question was reargued and resolved this year, with a liberal-conservative alignment that has long dominated state sovereign immunity cases.

* * * * *

In addition to the new main cases, the Supplement has notes on several other recent cases, including recent litigation on the Emoluments Clause. It also provides citations to recently published literature.

PERMISSION TO DUPLICATE

There are many intersections between **Federal Courts and the Law of Federal-State Relations** (8th ed. 2014) and Jeffries, Karlan, Low & Rutherglen, **Civil Rights Actions: Enforcing the Constitution** (3rd ed. 2013). A teacher using one book may wish to use material from the other book or its supplement. To facilitate such borrowings, we authorize teachers who have adopted either book to duplicate limited portions of the other or its annual supplement for distribution to their students. We are grateful to Foundation Press for agreeing to make this option available.

PWL
JCJJR
CAB

Charlottesville, Virginia
Durham, North Carolina
July, 2019

TABLE OF CONTENTS

PREFACE iii
TABLE OF CASES ix
TABLE OF AUTHORITIES xi

Casebook Page		Supplement Page
	CHAPTER I. CHOICE OF LAW IN THE FEDERAL SYSTEM	1
	Section 1. State Law in Federal Court	1
19	Additional Citation	1
25	Additional Citation	1
	Section 3. Supreme Court Review of State Court Decisions	1
88	Additional Citation	1
	CHAPTER II. THE POWER OF FEDERAL COURTS TO CREATE FEDERAL LAW	3
	Section 3. Rights of Action to Enforce Constitutional Rights	3
211	Replace Note 3 and the last paragraph of Note 2 with a new Note 3	3
	3. Applications of *Ziglar*	3
212	Add a new Note	4
	4A. Nationwide Injunctions	4
	Section 4. Customary International Law and the Alien Tort Statute	5
224	Additional Citations	5
242	Omit Note 3	5
248	Replace *Kiobel* and its Notes, pages 248–61, with a new Main Case and Notes	6
	Jesner v. Arab Bank, PLC	6
	Notes on *Jesner v. Arab Bank*	27
	1. Corporate ATS Liability	27
	2. *Kiobel* and the Presumption Against Extraterritoriality	28
	3. Questions and Comments on *Jesner v. Arab Bank*	29
	4. Bibliography	30
	CHAPTER III. JUDICIAL REVIEW AND JUSTICIABILITY	33
	Section 2. Standing	33
	Subsection A. Constitutional Core	33
306	Additional Citation	33

307	Additional Citation	33
	Subsection B. Statutory Standing	33
325	Additional Citation	33
326	Additional Citation	33
	Subsection D. Legislative and Governmental Standing	34
360	Add a new Note	34
	3A. *Virginia House of Delegates v. Bethune-Hill*	34
361	Additional Citation	37
361	Add new Notes	37
	4A. *Department of Commerce v. New York*	37
	4B. Recent Litigation Under the "Emoluments Clauses"	38
	(i) *Citizens for Responsibility and Ethics in Washington v. Trump*	39
	(ii) *District of Columbia v. Trump*	40
	(iii) *Blumenthal v. Trump*	42
	Section 3. Related Doctrines	43
	Subsection B. Ripeness	43
420	Omit footnote c (*Knick v. Township of Scott, Pennsylvania*)	43
	Section 4. The Political Question	43
470	Additional Citation	43
472	Replace Note 3 on Political Gerrymandering, pages 472–74, with a new Main Case and Note	44
	Rucho v. Common Cause	44
	Questions and Comments on *Rucho v. Common Cause*	69
	CHAPTER IV. CONGRESSIONAL CONTROL OF THE FEDERAL COURTS	71
	Section 1. Power to Limit Federal Court Jurisdiction	71
515	Additional Citation	71
515	Additional Citation	71
	Section 2. Power to Regulate Federal Rules of Decision and Judgments	71
547	Add a new Note	71
	10A. *Patchak v. Zinke*	71
	Section 4. Power to Create Non-Article III Courts	74
575	Additional Citation	74

614	Add new Notes..	74
	3A. Reaffirming the Public Rights Doctrine: *Oil States Energy Services, LLC v. Greene's Energy Group, LLC*...................	74
	3B. *Ortiz v. United States*	77
618	Add a new Note	78
	5A. *Lucia v. Securities and Exchange Commission*	78
619	Additional Citations	79

CHAPTER V. SUBJECT MATTER JURISDICTION 81

Section 2. Diversity Jurisdiction 81

732	*Home Depot U.S.A., Inc. v. Jackson*	81

Section 3. The Substance/Procedure Problem 81

757	Additional Citation	81

Section 4. Finality and Appellate Review 82

Subsection B. Circuit Court Review of District Court Decisions 82

800	*Hall v. Hall*; Additional Citations	82
806	Additional Citation	82

CHAPTER VI. ABSTENTION 83

Section 1. Introduction 83

809	*Gamble v. United States*	83

Section 2. *Younger* Abstention 83

827	Additional Citation	83

Section 6. International Comity Abstention 83

906	Additional Citation	83

CHAPTER VII. HABEAS CORPUS 85

Section 2. Review of State Court Decisions on the Merits: AEDPA 85

980	Additional Citation	85
986	Additional Citation	85
989	Add a new Note...	85
	3A. Decisions on the Merits Without Opinion	85
	(i) Federal Claim Rejected Because of Procedural Foreclosure: *Ylst v. Nunnemaker*	86
	(ii) Federal Claim Rejected on the Merits: *Wilson v. Sellers*	87
	(iii) Questions and Comments...	89

	Section 3. Procedural Limitations	90
	Subsection A. Procedural Foreclosure	90
1008	Additional Citation	90
	Section 4. Claims of Innocence	90
1050	Additional Citation	90
	Section 5. Intersecting Issues	90
	Subsection A. Applicability of *Teague* in State Courts	90
1051	Additional Citation	90
1054	Additional Citation	91

CHAPTER VIII. STATE SOVEREIGN IMMUNITY AND THE ELEVENTH AMENDMENT ... 93

	Section 1. Nature of the Limitation	93
1100	Add a new Note	93
	5A. Proper Terminology	93
1125	Add a new Note	94
	3A. Federal Injunctions to Enforce State Law: *Pennhurst State School and Hospital v. Halderman*	94
1129	Replace the Notes on the Intersection of the Eleventh Amendment and State Law, pages 1129–33, with a new Main Case and Notes	96
	Franchise Tax Board v. Hyatt	96
	Notes on *Franchise Tax Board v. Hyatt*	108
	1. *Nevada v. Hall*	108
	2. *Alden v. Maine*	109
	3. Questions and Comments on *Franchise Tax Board v. Hyatt*	110
	Section 2. Consent and Congressional Abrogation	110
1177	Additional Citation	110

CHAPTER IX. 42 U.S.C. § 1983 ... 111

	Section 2. Official Immunities	111
1274	Additional Citation	111
1274	Add a new Note	111
	11. Bibliography	111

TABLE OF CASES

The principal cases are in bold type.

Agostini v. Felton, 103
Alden v. Maine, 93, 99, 100, 102, 109
Alexander v. Sandoval, 10, 19
American Isuzu Motors, Inc. v. Ntsebeza, 12
Arar v. Ashcroft, 3
Argentine Republic v. Amerada Hess Shipping Corp., 23
Arizona State Legislature v. Arizona Independent Redistricting Commission, 56, 59
Atascadero State Hospital v. Scanlon, 95
Atlas Roofing Co. v. Occupational Safety and Health Review Comm'n, 76
Bakelite Corp., Ex parte, 76
Baker v. Carr, 45, 46
Bivens v. Six Unknown Fed. Narcotics Agents, 10
Blatchford v. Native Village of Noatak, 101
Blumenthal v. Trump, 42
California Democratic Party v. Jones, 61
Chester, Town of v. Laroe Estates, Inc., 56
Chisholm v. Georgia, 100
Church of Lukumi Babalu Aye, Inc. v. Hialeah, 67
Cissna v. Tennessee, 102
Citizens for Responsibility and Ethics in Washington v. Trump, 39
Colegrove v. Green, 46
Comptroller of Treasury of Md. v. Wynne, 86
Correctional Services Corp. v. Malesko, 10
Crowell v. Benson, 76
Daimler AG v. Bauman, 25
Davis v. Bandemer, 47, 48, 49, 50, 53
DeLovio v. Boit, 21
Department of Commerce v. New York, 37
District of Columbia v. Trump, 40
Doe v. Exxon Mobil Corp., 24
Edelman v. Jordan, 94
EEOC v. Arabian American Oil Co., 28
Elrod v. Burns, 61
Federal Maritime Comm'n v. South Carolina Ports Authority, 99
Franchise Tax Bd. of Cal. v. Hyatt (Hyatt I), 97
Franchise Tax Bd. of Cal. v. Hyatt (Hyatt II), 97, 101, 106
Franchise Tax Board v. Hyatt, 96
Free Enterprise Fund v. Public Company Accounting Oversight Board, 79
Freytag v. Commissioner, 78
Gaffney v. Cummings, 47, 63
Gamble v. United States, 83
Gill v. Whitford, 45, 51, 56, 68, 69
Gomillion v. Lightfoot, 47
Granfinanciera, S. A. v. Nordberg, 76
Hall v. Hall, 82
Hans v. Louisiana, 100
Harrington v. Richter, 88
Hernandez v. Mesa, 4
Hinderlider v. La Plata River & Cherry Creek Ditch Co., 102
Home Depot U.S.A., Inc. v. Jackson, 81
Hudson, United States v., 72
Hunt v. Cromartie, 47, 49
Jesner v. Arab Bank, PLC, 6
Johnson v. United States, 67
Kimbell Foods, Inc., United States v., 16
Kimble v. Marvel Entertainment, LLC, 106, 107
Kiobel v. Royal Dutch Petroleum Co., 7, 12, 13, 14, 16, 27, 28
Klein, United States v., 72
Knick v. Township of Scott, Pennsylvania, 43
Lamone v. Benisek, 45
League of United Latin American Citizens v. Perry, 47, 48
League of Women Voters of Florida v. Detzner, 57
Lucia v. Securities and Exchange Commission, 78
Marbury v. Madison, 45, 58, 69, 103
McCardle, Ex parte, 72
McCulloch v. Maryland, 98, 103
McIlvaine v. Coxe's Lessee, 99
Meyer v. Holley, 23
Michelin Tire Corp. v. Wages, 106
Miller v. Johnson, 52, 67
Mohamad v. Palestinian Authority, 11, 27
Morissette v. United States, 23
Morrison v. National Australia Bank Ltd., 28
Mossman v. Higginson, 20
Murray's Lessee v. Hoboken Land & Improvement Co., 76
Myers v. United States, 103
National City Bank of N.Y. v. Republic of China, 104

Table of Cases

Nevada v. Hall, 96, 97, 98, 100, 102, 103, 104, 105, 107, 108, 109, 110
New York, Ex parte, 101
Nixon v. Fitzgerald, 103
Nixon, United States v., 103
Oil States Energy Services, LLC v. Greene's Energy Group, LLC, 75
Ortiz v. United States, 77
Pacific States Telephone & Telegraph Co. v. Oregon, 56
Patchak v. Zinke, 71
Paton v. La Prade, 3
Pearson v. Callahan, 103
Pennhurst State School and Hospital v. Halderman, 94, 96
Petty v. Tennessee-Missouri Bridge Comm'n, 102
Planned Parenthood of Southeastern Pa. v. Casey, 106, 107
Plaut v. Spenthrift Farm, Inc., 72, 73
Principality of Monaco v. Mississippi, 100
Raines v. Byrd, 34, 35
Reynolds v. Sims, 61
Rhode Island v. Massachusetts, 102
Ron Pair Enterprises, Inc., United States v., 23
Rucho v. Common Cause, 44, 45
SAS Institute Inc. v. Iancu, 75
Schooner Exchange v. McFaddon, 99
SEC v. Chenery Corp., 85
Seminole Tribe of Florida v. Florida, 93
Shaw v. Reno, 46, 52
Sixty-seventh Minnesota State Senate v. Beens, 35
Smith v. Reeves, 101
Sosa v. Alvarez-Machain, 8, 9, 10, 11, 16, 17, 18, 19, 20, 21, 22, 24, 29
Texas Industries, Inc. v. Radcliff Materials, Inc., 102
Textile Workers v. Lincoln Mills of Ala., 16
The Nereide, 20
The Paquete Habana, 20
Trainmen v. Toledo, P. & W. R., Co., 72
Trump v. Hawaii, 5
Tun-Cos v. Perrotte, 3
Vance v. Rumsfeld, 3
Vanderklok v. TSA, 3
Vieth v. Jubelirer, 45, 47, 48, 49, 50, 51, 54, 55, 56, 59, 61, 63
Virginia House of Delegates v. Bethune-Hill, 34
Washington v. Davis, 67
Wesberry v. Sanders, 46, 47
Williams v. United States, 76
Wilson v. Sellers, 85, 87
Wood v. Broom, 46
World-Wide Volkswagen Corp. v. Woodson, 101

Wright v. Rockefeller, 47
Ylst v. Nunnemaker, 86
Young, Ex parte, 94
Ziglar v. Abbasi, 10

TABLE OF AUTHORITIES

Alford, Roger P., Human Rights After *Kiobel*: Choice of Law and the Rise of Transnational Tort Litigation, 63 Emory L.J. 1089 (2014), 31

Alford, Roger P., The Future of Human Rights Litigation After *Kiobel*, 89 Notre Dame L. Rev. 749 (2014), 31

Amdur, Spencer E. and David Hausman, Nationwide Injunctions and Nationwide Harm, 131 Harv. L. Rev. F. 49 (2017), 5

Baude, William, Is Qualified Immunity Unlawful?, 106 Calif. L. Rev. 45 (2018), 111

Baude, William, Sovereign Immunity and the Constitutional Text, 103 Va. L. Rev. 1 (2017), 109

Baude, William, Standing in the Shadow of Congress, 2016 Sup. Ct. Rev. 197, 33

Beck, Randy, Qui Tam Litigation Against Government Officials: Constitutional Implications of a Neglected History, 93 Notre Dame L. Rev. 1235 (2018), 33

Bellia, Anthony J. Jr. and Bradford R. Clark, The Alien Tort Statute and the Law of Nations, 78 U. Chi. L. Rev. 445 (2011), 18, 30

Bellia, Anthony J. Jr. and Bradford R. Clark, The Law of Nations and the United States Constitution (2017), 5

Bellia, Anthony J. Jr. and Bradford R. Clark, Two Myths About the Alien Tort Statute, 89 Notre Dame L. Rev. 1609 (2014), 31

Bellia, Anthony J. Jr. and Bradford R. Clark, Why Federal Courts Apply the Law of Nations Even Though It Is Not the Supreme Law of the Land, 106 Georgetown L.J. 1915 (2018), 5

Birk, Daniel D., The Common-Law Exceptions Clause: Congressional Control of Supreme Court Appellate Jurisdiction in Light of British Precedent, 63 Vill. L. Rev. 189 (2018), 71

Blum, Karen M., Qualified Immunity: Time to Change the Message, 93 Notre Dame L. Rev. 1887 (2018), 111

Borchers, Patrick J., Is the Supreme Court Really Going to Regulate Choice of Law Involving States?, 50 Creighton L. Rev. 7 (2016), 109

Bradley, Curtis A. and Jack L. Goldsmith, Customary International Law as Federal Common Law: A Critique of the Modern Position, 110 Harv. L. Rev. 815 (1997), 20

Bradley, Curtis A., State Action and Corporate Human Rights Liability, 85 Notre Dame L. Rev. 1823 (2010), 30

Bradley, Curtis A., The Alien Tort Statute and Article III, 42 Va. J. Int'l L. 587 (2002), 30

Bray, Samuel L., Multiple Chancellors: Reforming the National Injunction, 131 Harv. L. Rev. 417 (2017), 5

Brown, George D., "Counter-Counter-Terrorism via Lawsuit"—The *Bivens* Impasse, 82 S. Calif. L. Rev. 841 (2009), 3

Bruhl, Aaron-Andrew P., One Good Plaintiff is Not Enough, 67 Duke L.J. 481 (2017), 33

Bryant, Graham K., The Historical Argument for State Sovereign Immunity in Bankruptcy Proceedings, 87 Miss. L.J. 49 (2018), 110

Burbank, Stephen B. and Tobias Barrington Wolfe, Class Actions, Statutes of Limitation and Repose, and Federal Common Law, 167 U. Pa. L. Rev. 1 (2018), 1

Cassel, Doug, Corporate Aiding and Abetting of Human Rights Violations: Confusion in the Courts, 6 Nw. U. J. Int'l Hum. Rts. 304 (2008), 30

Cassell, Doug, Suing Americans for Human Rights Torts Overseas: The Supreme Court Leaves the Door Open, 89 Notre Dame L. Rev. 1773 (2014), 31

Casto, William R., The ATS Cause of Action is *Sui Generis*, 89 Notre Dame L. Rev. 1545 (2014), 31

Chen, Alan K., The Intractability of Qualified Immunity, 93 Notre Dame L. Rev. 1937 (2018), 111

Clark, Bradford R., Federal Common Law: A Structural Reinterpretation, 144 U. Pa. L. Rev. 1245 (1996), 102

Clopton, Zachary D., Justiciability, Federalism, and the Administrative State, 103 Cornell L. Rev. 1431 (2018), 79

Crocker, Katherine Mims, Qualified Immunity and Constitutional Structure, 117 Mich. L. Rev. 1405 (2019), 111

Davis, Seth and Christopher A. Whytock, State Remedies for Human Rights, 98 B.U. L. Rev. 397 (2018), 31

Deutsch, Ruthanne M., Federalizing Retroactivity Rules: The Unrealized Promise of *Danforth v. Minnesota* and the Unmet Obligation of State Courts to Vindicate Federal Constitutional Rights, 44 Fla. St. U. L. Rev. 53 (2016), 91

Dodge, William S., Alien Tort Statute Litigation: The Road Not Taken, 89 Notre Dame L. Rev. 1577 (2014), 31

Dodge, William S., Customary International Law, Change, and the Constitution, 106 Georgetown L.J. 1559 (2018), 5

Dodge, William S., The Constitutionality of the Alien Tort Statute: Some Observations on Text and Context, 42 Va. J. Int'l L. 687 (2002), 30

Dorf, Michael D., Congressional Power to Strip State Courts of Jurisdiction, 97 Tex. L. Rev. 1 (2018), 71

Epps, Daniel, Harmless Errors and Substantial Rights, 131 Harv. L. Rev. 2117 (2018), 85

Field, Martha, The Eleventh Amendment and Other Sovereign Immunity Doctrines: Congressional Imposition of Suit upon the States, 126 U. Pa. L. Rev. 1203 (1978), 95

Frost, Amanda, In Defense of Nationwide Injunctions, 93 N.Y.U. L. Rev. 1065 (2018), 5

Gardner, Maggie, Abstention at the Border, 105 Va. L. Rev. 63 (2019), 83

Golove, David M. and Daniel J. Hulsebosch, The Law of Nations and the Constitution: An Early Modern Perspective, 106 Georgetown L.J. 1593 (2018), 5

Harrison, John, The Constitution and the Law of Nations, 106 Georgetown L.J. 1659 (2018), 5

Harrison, John, The Political Question Doctrines, 67 Am. U. L. Rev. 457 (2017), 43

Hessick, F. Andrew, Consenting to Adjudication Outside the Article III Courts, 71 Vand. L. Rev. 715 (2018), 79

Keitner, Chimene, Conceptualizing Complicity in Alien Tort Cases, 60 Hastings L.J. 61 (2008), 30

Kontorovich, Eugene, *Kiobel* Surprise: Unexpected by Scholars but Consistent with International Trends, 89 Notre Dame L. Rev. 1671 (2014), 31

Kovarsky, Lee, Structural Change in State Postconviction Review, 93 Notre Dame L. Rev. 443 (2017), 90

Ku, Julian G., The Curious Case of Corporate Liability Under the Alien Tort Statute: A Flawed System of Judicial Lawmaking, 51 Va. J. Int'l L. 353 (2011), 30

Lammon, Bryan, Finality, Appealability, and the Scope of Interlocutory Review, 93 Wash. L. Rev. 1809 (2018), 82

Lammon, Bryan, *Hall v. Hall*: A Lose-Lose Case for Appellate Jurisdiction, 68 Emory L.J. Online 1001 (2018), 82

Lee, Thomas H., The Law of Nations and the Judicial Branch, 106 Georgetown L.J. 1707 (2018), 5

Lee, Thomas H., The Safe-Conduct Theory of the Alien Tort Statute, 106 Colum. L. Rev. 830 (2006), 21

Lee, Thomas H., Three Lives of the Alien Tort Statute: The Evolving Role of the Judiciary in U.S. Foreign Relations, 89 Notre Dame L. Rev. 1645 (2014), 31

Litman, Leah M., Legal Innocence and Federal Habeas, 104 Va. L. Rev. 417 (2018), 90

Mank, Bradford C., State Standing in *United States v. Texas*: Opening the Floodgates to States Challenging the Federal Government, or Proper Federalism?, 2018 U. Ill. L. Rev. 211, 37

Margulies, Peter, Judging Myopia in Hindsight: *Bivens* Actions, National Security Decisions and the Rule of Law, 96 Iowa L. Rev. 195 (2010), 3

Michelman, Scott, The Branch Best Qualified to Abolish Immunity, 93 Notre Dame L. Rev. 1999 (2018), 111

Morley, Michael T., Nationwide Injunctions, Rule 23(B)(2), and the Remedial Powers of the Lower Courts, 97 B.U. L. Rev. 615 (2017), 5

Nelson, Caleb, Sovereign Immunity as a Doctrine of Personal Jurisdiction, 115 Harv. L. Rev. 1559 (2002), 99

Nielson, Aaron L. and Christopher J. Walker, A Qualified Defense of Qualified Immunity, 93 Notre Dame L. Rev. 1853 (2018), 111

Pernell, LeRoy, Racial Justice and Federal Habeas Corpus as Postconviction Relief from State Convictions, 69 Mercer L. Rev. 453 (2018), 85

Pfander, James E., Rethinking the Supreme Court's Original Jurisdiction in State-Party Cases, 82 Cal. L. Rev. 555 (1994), 99

Pfander, James E., Standing, Litigable Interests, and Article III's Case-or-Controversy Requirement, 65 UCLA L. Rev. 170 (2018), 33

Preis, John F., Qualified Immunity and Fault, 93 Notre Dame L. Rev. 1969 (2018), 111

Primus, Eve Brensike, Federal Review of State Criminal Convictions: A Structural Approach to Adequacy Doctrine, 116 Mich. L. Rev. 75 (2017), 90

Ramsey, Michael D., International Law Limits on Investor Liability in Human Rights Litigation, 50 Harv. Int'l L.J. 271 (2009), 30

Ramsey, Michael D., The Constitution's Text and Customary International Law, 106 Georgetown L.J. 1747 (2018), 5

Reinert, Alexander A., Qualified Immunity at Trial, 93 Notre Dame L. Rev. 2065 (2018), 111

Rensberger, Jeffrey L., The Metasplit: The Law Applied After Transfer in Federal Question Cases, 2018 Wis. L. Rev. 847, 1

Schwartz, Joanna C., The Case Against Qualified Immunity, 93 Notre Dame L. Rev. 1797 (2018), 111

Shapiro, David M. and Charles Hogle, The Horror Chamber: Unqualified Immunity in Prison, 93 Notre Dame L. Rev. 2021 (2018), 111

Shapiro, David, Comment, Wrong Turns: The Eleventh Amendment and the *Pennhurst* Case, 98 Harv. L. Rev. 61 (1984), 95

Siddique, Zayn, Nationwide Injunctions, 117 Colum. L. Rev. 2095 (2017), 5

Smith, Fred O. Jr., Abstention in the Time of Ferguson, 131 Harv. L. Rev. 2283 (2018), 83

Smith, Fred O. Jr., Formalism, Ferguson, and the Future of Qualified Immunity, 93 Notre Dame L. Rev. 2093 (2018), 111

Spencer, A. Benjamin, Substance, Procedure, and the Rules Enabling Act, 66 U.C.L.A. L. Rev. 654 (2019), 81

Steinhardt, Ralph G., Determining Which Human Rights Claims "Touch and Concern" the United States: Justice Kennedy's *Filartiga*, 89 Notre Dame L. Rev. 1695 (2014), 31

Stephan, Paul B., Inferences of Judicial Lawmaking Power and the Law of Nations, 106 Georgetown L.J. 1793 (2018), 5

Stephens, Beth, The Curious History of the Alien Tort Statute, 89 Notre Dame L. Rev. 1467 (2014), 31

Sykes, Alan O., Corporate Liability for Extraterritorial Torts Under the Alien Tort Statute and Beyond: An Economic Analysis, 100 Georgetown L.J. 2161 (2012), 30

Vázquez, Carlos M., Things We Do with Presumptions: Reflections on *Kiobel v. Royal Dutch Petroleum*, 89 Notre Dame L. Rev. 1719 (2014), 31

Vladeck, Stephen I., National Security and *Bivens* After *Iqbal*, 14 Lewis & Clark L. Rev. 255 (2010), 3

Wells, Michael L., Qualified Immunity After *Ziglar v. Abbasi*: The Case for a Categorical Approach, 68 Am. U. L. Rev. 379 (2018), 111

Wells, Michael L., Wrongful Convictions, Constitutional Remedies, and *Nelson v. Colorado*, 86 Fordham L. Rev. 2199 (2018), 1

Woolhandler, Ann, Interstate Sovereign Immunity, 2006 Sup. Ct. Rev. 249, 99, 109

Wuerth, Ingrid, The Future of the Federal Common Law of Foreign Relations, 106 Georgetown L.J. 1825 (2018), 5

Young, Ernest A., Sorting Out the Debate Over Customary International Law, 42 Va. J. Int'l L. 365 (2002), 20

Young, Ernest A., Universal Jurisdiction, the Alien Tort Statute, and Transnational Public

Law Litigation After *Kiobel*, 64
Duke L.J. 1023 (2015), 30

UNIVERSITY CASEBOOK SERIES®

2019 SUPPLEMENT TO

Federal Courts and the Law of Federal-State Relations

NINTH EDITION

1981 SUPPLEMENT TO
FEDERAL COURTS
AND THE LAW OF
FEDERAL-STATE
RELATIONS

CHAPTER I

CHOICE OF LAW IN THE FEDERAL SYSTEM

SECTION 1. STATE LAW IN FEDERAL COURT

Page 19, add at the end of footnote k:

Compare the analysis of the source of law that should govern the tolling of statutes of limitations in federal class action litigation in Stephen B. Burbank and Tobias Barrington Wolfe, Class Actions, Statutes of Limitation and Repose, and Federal Common Law, 167 U. Pa. L. Rev. 1 (2018). The authors conclude that:

> Careful attention to the source of the tolling rule applied in [prior cases], to sources of authority for federal law, and to the distinction between sources of authority and sources of rules, leads us to reaffirm that the tolling rule announced [by the Supreme Court] is a rule of federal common law. . . . Rule 23 [of the Federal Rules of Civil Procedure] is not the source [of the] tolling [principle], but it is the source of the procedural policies that the federal courts are carrying into effect through their authority to promulgate federal common law.

Page 25, add at the end of footnote b:

See also Jeffrey L. Rensberger, The Metasplit: The Law Applied After Transfer in Federal Question Cases, 2018 Wis. L. Rev. 847.

SECTION 3. SUPREME COURT REVIEW OF STATE COURT DECISIONS

Page 88, add at the end of footnote a:

For a unique and interesting suggested application of *Brand*, see Michael L. Wells, Wrongful Convictions, Constitutional Remedies, and *Nelson v. Colorado*, 86 Fordham L. Rev. 2199, 2210–15 (2018).

CHAPTER II

THE POWER OF FEDERAL COURTS TO CREATE FEDERAL LAW

SECTION 3. RIGHTS OF ACTION TO ENFORCE CONSTITUTIONAL RIGHTS

Page 211, replace Note 3 and the last paragraph of Note 2 with a new Note 3:

3. APPLICATIONS OF *ZIGLAR*

Ziglar v. Abbasi was a divided decision rendered by a six-Justice Court.[c] At the time, its significance might have been doubted, but subsequent decisions have made its restrictive potential plain. In Vanderklok v. TSA, 868 F.3d 189 (3d Cir. 2017), and Tun-Cos v. Perrotte, 922 F.3d 514 (4th Cir. 2019), the Courts of Appeal used the combination of "new context" and "special factors counselling hesitation" to preclude *Bivens* actions in circumstances where they once would have been thought straightforward.

Vanderklok involved an airline passenger who had an unfortunate encounter with a TSA screener. The passenger announced his intention to file a complaint, whereupon the screener called the Philadelphia police and had him arrested for bringing a bomb to the airport. The passenger was tried and acquitted of all charges, then brought a *Bivens* action claiming retaliatory prosecution in violation of the First Amendment. Such claims had been permitted before, see, e.g., Paton v. La Prade, 524 F.2d 862 (3d Cir. 1975), but the Third Circuit concluded that airport-security screening was a "new context" for which *Bivens* claims were not available. The "national security implications" of that context constituted "special factors counselling hesitation."

Similar reasoning applied in *Tun-Cos v. Perrotte*, which involved Fourth Amendment claims brought by Latino men against Immigration and Customs Enforcement agents. Even though *Bivens* itself involved a Fourth Amendment claim, the Fourth Circuit found that claims against ICE agents, who enforce immigration statutes rather than the criminal law, was a "new

---

[c] Lower court decisions prior to *Ziglar* invoked "special factors counselling hesitation" to deny *Bivens* actions relating to the "war on terror" or military actions. See, e.g., Vance v. Rumsfeld, 701 F.3d 193 (7th Cir. 2012) (en banc) (rejecting *Bivens* claims by U.S. citizens allegedly tortured in Iraq); Arar v. Ashcroft, 585 F.3d 599 (2d Cir. 2009) (en banc) (rejecting *Bivens* claims by noncitizens for alleged mistreatment in Syria). Academic opinion had been more supportive. See, e.g., Stephen I. Vladeck, National Security and *Bivens* After Iqbal, 14 Lewis & Clark L. Rev. 255 (2010); George D. Brown, "Counter-Counter-Terrorism via Lawsuit"—The *Bivens* Impasse, 82 S. Calif. L. Rev. 841 (2009); Peter Margulies, Judging Myopia in Hindsight: *Bivens* Actions, National Security Decisions and the Rule of Law, 96 Iowa L. Rev. 195 (2010).

context" involving "special factors counselling hesitation." The court's articulation of that inquiry shows how restrictive it has become: "In determining whether 'special factors' are present, we focus on whether Congress *might doubt* the need for an implied damages remedy." (Emphasis in original.) The fact that Congress had legislated in the area without providing a damages remedy against ICE agents was enough.

Vanderklok and *Tun-Cos* suggest that the restrictive potential of *Ziglar* has been fully realized. Almost any difference suffices to make a context "new," which triggers an inquiry into "special factors." Those factors include not only persuasive arguments against *Bivens* actions but also any concerns that Congress *might* think persuasive. The door is almost closed

The issue is now before the Supreme Court. Hernandez v. Mesa, 885 F.3d 811 (5th Cir. 2018), was originally before the Court on the Fifth Circuit's grant of qualified immunity to a Customs & Border Patrol Agent accused of fatally shooting a Mexican teenager just across the border in Mexico. The case was pending at the time of *Ziglar* and was remanded for reconsideration in light of that decision. On remand, the Fifth Circuit, sitting en banc, found that the "transnational aspect of the facts presents a 'new context' under *Bivens*," resulting in no cause of action. Certiorari has been granted and presumably the Supreme Court will review that decision during its 2019 Term.

Page 212, add a new Note after Note 4:

4A. NATIONWIDE INJUNCTIONS

The *Bivens* line of cases concerns only the ability to sue for damages. It is well accepted that private parties may seek prospective relief to stop federal government action violative of federal law, assuming they meet standing and other justiciability requirements. In recent years, however, there has been much discussion of the propriety of nationwide federal-court injunctions that have the effect of halting executive-branch programs or activities throughout the country. When issued in cases that have not been certified as class actions, these injunctions affect government interactions with many individuals who are not before the court.

For example, in 2015, a federal district court judge in Texas issued a nationwide injunction against President Obama's Deferred Action for Parents of Americans and Lawful Permanent Residents (DAPA) program that would have given many aliens who were illegally present in the United States an exemption from deportation and access to a renewable work permit. And in 2017 several federal district courts issued nationwide injunctions against President Trump's "travel ban" orders that were designed to restrict the ability of individuals from certain countries to enter the United States.

Critics contend that such injunctions give individual district court judges too much authority to affect national policy, lead to forum shopping by plaintiffs, unduly politicize the judiciary, and prevent the useful percolation of issues among the circuits prior to potential Supreme Court review. They also contend that such injunctions are a modern phenomenon that is inconsistent with historical understandings of the proper scope of equitable relief. See, for example, Samuel L. Bray, Multiple Chancellors: Reforming the National Injunction, 131 Harv. L. Rev. 417 (2017).

Defenders of district court discretion to issue such injunctions contend that they are sometimes needed either to provide a plaintiff with complete relief, because the rights being asserted are not divisible, or to avoid undue confusion in the implementation of federal programs. Such injunctions are also claimed to promote rule-of-law values by ensuring that individuals who are in similar situations are treated the same by the government as those before the court. See, for example, Amanda Frost, In Defense of Nationwide Injunctions, 93 N.Y.U. L. Rev. 1065 (2018).

In Trump v. Hawaii, 585 U.S. ___, 138 S.Ct. 2392 (2018), the Supreme Court reversed a nationwide preliminary injunction in the travel ban litigation. But it did so because it found that the plaintiffs had not established a likelihood of success on the merits, and thus it did not address the general propriety of this form of relief. Justice Thomas wrote a concurrence, however, that specifically questioned nationwide injunctions, which he referred to as "universal injunctions." Relying heavily on Bray's article and other scholarship, Thomas reasoned that nothing in either existing statutes or in the inherent equitable authority of the federal courts provides support for universal injunctions, and that such injunctions are inconsistent with "traditional limits on equity and judicial power."

For additional discussion of these issues, see Spencer E. Amdur & David Hausman, Nationwide Injunctions and Nationwide Harm, 131 Harv. L. Rev. F. 49 (2017); Michael T. Morley, Nationwide Injunctions, Rule 23(B)(2), and the Remedial Powers of the Lower Courts, 97 B.U. L. Rev. 615 (2017); Zayn Siddique, Nationwide Injunctions, 117 Colum. L. Rev. 2095 (2017).

SECTION 4. CUSTOMARY INTERNATIONAL LAW AND THE ALIEN TORT STATUTE

Page 224, add a footnote at the end of the second full paragraph:

e   Anthony J. Bellia Jr. and Bradford R. Clark, The Law of Nations and the United States Constitution (2017), reflects the authors' views on these issues relating to the domestic status of the law of nations. This book was the subject of a 2018 symposium in the Georgetown Law Journal. See William S. Dodge, Customary International Law, Change, and the Constitution, 106 Georgetown L.J. 1559 (2018); David M. Golove and Daniel J. Hulsebosch, The Law of Nations and the Constitution: An Early Modern Perspective, 106 Georgetown L.J. 1593 (2018); John Harrison, The Constitution and the Law of Nations, 106 Georgetown L.J. 1659 (2018); Thomas H. Lee, The Law of Nations and the Judicial Branch, 106 Georgetown L.J. 1707 (2018); Michael D. Ramsey, The Constitution's Text and Customary International Law, 106 Georgetown L.J. 1747 (2018); Paul B. Stephan, Inferences of Judicial Lawmaking Power and the Law of Nations, 106 Georgetown L.J. 1793 (2018); Ingrid Wuerth, The Future of the Federal Common Law of Foreign Relations, 106 Georgetown L.J. 1825 (2018). A response to these articles can be found in Anthony J. Bellia Jr. and Bradford R. Clark, Why Federal Courts Apply the Law of Nations Even Though It Is Not the Supreme Law of the Land, 106 Georgetown L.J. 1915 (2018).

Page 242, omit Note 3:

[Explanation: Topic covered in next Main Case and Notes.]

Page 248, replace *Kiobel* and its Notes, pages 248–61, with a new Main Case and Notes:

Jesner v. Arab Bank, PLC

Supreme Court of the United States, 2018.
584 U.S. ___, 138 S.Ct. 1386.

■ JUSTICE KENNEDY announced the judgment of the Court and delivered the opinion of the Court with respect to Parts I, II-B-1, and II-C, and an opinion with respect to Parts II-A, II-B-2, II-B-3, and III, in which THE CHIEF JUSTICE and JUSTICE THOMAS join.

Petitioners in this case, or the persons on whose behalf petitioners now assert claims, allegedly were injured or killed by terrorist acts committed abroad. Those terrorist acts, it is contended, were in part caused or facilitated by a foreign corporation. Petitioners now seek to impose liability on the foreign corporation for the conduct of its human agents, including its then-chairman and other high-ranking management officials. The suits were filed in a United States District Court under the Alien Tort Statute, commonly referred to as the ATS. See 28 U.S.C. § 1350.

The foreign corporation charged with liability in these ATS suits is Arab Bank, PLC; and it is respondent here. Some of Arab Bank's officials, it is alleged, allowed the Bank to be used to transfer funds to terrorist groups in the Middle East, which in turn enabled or facilitated criminal acts of terrorism, causing the deaths or injuries for which petitioners now seek compensation. Petitioners seek to prove Arab Bank helped the terrorists receive the moneys in part by means of currency clearances and bank transactions passing through its New York City offices, all by means of electronic transfers.

It is assumed here that those individuals who inflicted death or injury by terrorism committed crimes in violation of well-settled, fundamental precepts of international law, precepts essential for basic human-rights protections. It is assumed as well that individuals who knowingly and purposefully facilitated banking transactions to aid, enable, or facilitate the terrorist acts would themselves be committing crimes under the same international-law prohibitions.

Petitioners contend that international and domestic laws impose responsibility and liability on a corporation if its human agents use the corporation to commit crimes in violation of international laws that protect human rights. The question here is whether the Judiciary has the authority, in an ATS action, to make that determination and then to enforce that liability in ATS suits, all without any explicit authorization from Congress to do so.

The answer turns upon the proper interpretation and implementation of the ATS. The statute provides: "The district courts shall have original jurisdiction of any civil action by an alien for a tort only, committed in violation of the law of nations or a treaty of the United States." § 1350. The Court must first ask whether the law of nations imposes liability on corporations for human-rights violations committed by its employees. The Court must also ask whether it has authority and discretion in an ATS suit to impose liability on a corporation without a specific direction from Congress to do so.

I

A

... During the pendency of this litigation, there was an unrelated case that also implicated the issue whether the ATS is applicable to suits in this country against foreign corporations. See Kiobel v. Royal Dutch Petroleum Co., 621 F.3d 111 (2d Cir. 2010). That suit worked its way through the trial court and the Court of Appeals for the Second Circuit. The *Kiobel* litigation did not involve banking transactions. Its allegations were that holding companies incorporated in the Netherlands and the United Kingdom had, through a Nigerian subsidiary, aided and abetted the Nigerian Government in human-rights abuses. In *Kiobel*, the Court of Appeals held that the ATS does not extend to suits against corporations. This Court granted certiorari in *Kiobel*.

After additional briefing and reargument in *Kiobel*, this Court held that, given all the circumstances, the suit could not be maintained under the ATS. Kiobel v. Royal Dutch Petroleum Co., 569 U.S. 108, 114, 124–25 (2013). The rationale of the holding, however, was not that the ATS does not extend to suits against foreign corporations. That question was left unresolved. The Court ruled, instead, that "all the relevant conduct took place outside the United States." Dismissal of the action was required based on the presumption against extraterritorial application of statutes.

So while this Court in *Kiobel* affirmed the ruling that the action there could not be maintained, it did not address the broader holding of the Court of Appeals that dismissal was required because corporations may not be sued under the ATS. Still, the courts of the Second Circuit deemed that broader holding to be binding precedent. As a consequence, in the instant case the District Court dismissed petitioners' ATS claims based on the earlier *Kiobel* holding in the Court of Appeals; and on review of the dismissal order the Court of Appeals, also adhering to its earlier holding, affirmed. This Court granted certiorari in the instant case.

Since the Court of Appeals relied on its *Kiobel* holding in the instant case, it is instructive to begin with an analysis of that decision. The majority opinion in *Kiobel*, written by Judge Cabranes, held that the ATS does not apply to alleged international-law violations by a corporation. Judge Cabranes relied in large part on the fact that international criminal tribunals have consistently limited their jurisdiction to natural persons.

Judge Leval filed a separate opinion. He concurred in the judgment on other grounds but disagreed with the proposition that the foreign corporation was not subject to suit under the ATS. Judge Leval conceded that "international law, of its own force, imposes no liabilities on corporations or other private juridical entities." But he reasoned that corporate liability for violations of international law is an issue of "civil compensatory liability" that international law leaves to individual nations. Later decisions in the Courts of Appeals for the Seventh, Ninth, and District of Columbia Circuits agreed with Judge Leval and held that corporations can be subject to suit under the ATS. The respective opinions by Judges Cabranes and Leval are scholarly and extensive, providing significant guidance for this Court in the case now before it.

With this background, it is now proper to turn to the history of the ATS and the decisions interpreting it.

B

[In this section of its opinion, the Court reviewed the history of the ATS as recounted in Sosa v. Alvarez-Machain, 542 U.S. 692 (2004). It also described the evolution of ATS litigation from *Filartiga* to *Kiobel*.]

II

With these principles in mind, this Court now must decide whether common-law liability under the ATS extends to a foreign corporate defendant. It could be argued, under the Court's holding in *Kiobel*, that even if, under accepted principles of international law and federal common law, corporations are subject to ATS liability for human-rights crimes committed by their human agents, in this case the activities of the defendant corporation and the alleged actions of its employees have insufficient connections to the United States to subject it to jurisdiction under the ATS. Various amici urge this as a rationale to affirm here, while the Government argues that the Court should remand this case so the Court of Appeals can address the issue in the first instance. There are substantial arguments on both sides of that question; but it is not the question on which this Court granted certiorari, nor is it the question that has divided the Courts of Appeals.

The question whether foreign corporations are subject to liability under the ATS should be addressed; for, if there is no liability for Arab Bank, the lengthy and costly litigation concerning whether corporate contacts like those alleged here suffice to impose liability would be pointless. In addition, a remand to the Court of Appeals would require prolonging litigation that already has caused significant diplomatic tensions with Jordan for more than a decade. So it is proper for this Court to decide whether corporations, or at least foreign corporations, are subject to liability in an ATS suit filed in a United States district court.

Before recognizing a common-law action under the ATS, federal courts must apply the test announced in *Sosa*. An initial, threshold question is whether a plaintiff can demonstrate that the alleged violation is "of a norm that is specific, universal, and obligatory." 542 U.S. at 732. And even assuming that, under international law, there is a specific norm that can be controlling, it must be determined further whether allowing this case to proceed under the ATS is a proper exercise of judicial discretion, or instead whether caution requires the political branches to grant specific authority before corporate liability can be imposed. See id. at 732–33 and nn. 20–21. "[T]he potential implications for the foreign relations of the United States of recognizing such causes should make courts particularly wary of impinging on the discretion of the Legislative and Executive Branches in managing foreign affairs." Id. at 727.

It must be said that some of the considerations that pertain to determining whether there is a specific, universal, and obligatory norm that is established under international law are applicable as well in determining whether deference must be given to the political branches. For instance, the fact that the charters of some international tribunals and the provisions of some congressional statutes addressing international human-rights violations are specifically limited to individual wrongdoers, and thus foreclose corporate liability, has significant bearing both on the content of the norm being asserted and the question whether courts should defer to Congress. The two inquiries inform each other and are, to that extent, not altogether discrete.

With that introduction, it is proper now to turn first to the question whether there is an international-law norm imposing liability on corporations for acts of their employees that contravene fundamental human rights.

A

Petitioners and Arab Bank disagree as to whether corporate liability is a question of international law or only a question of judicial authority and discretion under domestic law. [At this point the Court considered various materials relating to corporate liability under international law.]

[T]he Court need not resolve the questions whether corporate liability is a question that is governed by international law, or, if so, whether international law imposes liability on corporations. There is at least sufficient doubt on the point to turn to *Sosa*'s second question—whether the Judiciary must defer to Congress, allowing it to determine in the first instance whether that universal norm has been recognized and, if so, whether it is prudent and necessary to direct its enforcement in suits under the ATS.

B

1

Sosa is consistent with this Court's general reluctance to extend judicially created private rights of action. The Court's recent precedents cast doubt on the authority of courts to extend or create private causes of action even in the realm of domestic law, where this Court has "recently and repeatedly said that a decision to create a private right of action is one better left to legislative judgment in the great majority of cases." 542 U.S. at 727 (citing Correctional Services Corp. v. Malesko, 534 U.S. 61, 68 (2001); Alexander v. Sandoval, 532 U.S. 275, 286–87 (2001)). That is because "the Legislature is in the better position to consider if the public interest would be served by imposing a new substantive legal liability." Ziglar v. Abbasi, 582 U.S. ___, ___, 137 S.Ct. 1843, 1857 (2017). Thus, "if there are sound reasons to think Congress might doubt the efficacy or necessity of a damages remedy, . . . courts must refrain from creating the remedy in order to respect the role of Congress." Id. at ___, 137 S.Ct. at 1858.

This caution extends to the question whether the courts should exercise the judicial authority to mandate a rule that imposes liability upon artificial entities like corporations. Thus, in *Malesko* the Court held that corporate defendants may not be held liable in *Bivens* actions. See Bivens v. Six Unknown Fed. Narcotics Agents, 403 U.S. 388 (1971). Allowing corporate liability would have been a "marked extension" of *Bivens* that was unnecessary to advance its purpose of holding individual officers responsible for "engaging in unconstitutional wrongdoing." *Malesko*, 534 U.S. at 74. Whether corporate defendants should be subject to suit was "a question for Congress, not us, to decide." Id. at 72.

Neither the language of the ATS nor the precedents interpreting it support an exception to these general principles in this context. In fact, the separation-of-powers concerns that counsel against courts creating private rights of action apply with particular force in the context of the ATS. The political branches, not the Judiciary, have the responsibility and institutional capacity to weigh foreign-policy concerns. That the ATS implicates foreign relations "is itself a reason for a high bar to new private causes of action for violating international law." *Sosa*, 542 U.S. at 727.

In *Sosa*, the Court emphasized that federal courts must exercise "great caution" before recognizing new forms of liability under the ATS. In light of the foreign-policy and separation-of-powers concerns inherent in ATS litigation, there is an argument that a proper application of *Sosa* would preclude courts from ever recognizing any new causes of action under the ATS. But the Court need not resolve that question in this case. Either way, absent further action from Congress it would be inappropriate for courts to extend ATS liability to foreign corporations.

2

Even in areas less fraught with foreign-policy consequences, the Court looks to analogous statutes for guidance on the appropriate boundaries of judge-made causes of action. Doing so is even more important in the realm of international law, where "the general practice has been to look for legislative guidance before exercising innovative authority over substantive law." *Sosa*, 542 U.S. at 726.

Here, the logical place to look for a statutory analogy to an ATS common-law action is the [Torture Victim Protection Act (TVPA)]—the only cause of action under the ATS created by Congress rather than the courts. . . .

The key feature of the TVPA for this case is that it limits liability to "individuals," which, the Court has held, unambiguously limits liability to natural persons. Mohamad v. Palestinian Authority, 566 U.S. 449, 453–56 (2012). Congress's decision to exclude liability for corporations in actions brought under the TVPA is all but dispositive of the present case. That decision illustrates that significant foreign-policy implications require the courts to draw a careful balance in defining the scope of actions under the ATS. It would be inconsistent with that balance to create a remedy broader than the one created by Congress. Indeed, it "would be remarkable to take a more aggressive role in exercising a jurisdiction that remained largely in shadow for much of the prior two centuries." Sosa, 542 U.S. at 726. . . .

Petitioners contend that, instead of the TVPA, the most analogous statute here is the Anti-Terrorism Act. That Act does permit suits against corporate entities. See 18 U.S.C. §§ 2331(3), 2333(d)(2). In fact, in these suits some of the foreign plaintiffs joined their claims to those of United States nationals suing Arab Bank under the Anti-Terrorism Act. But the Anti-Terrorism Act provides a cause of action only to "national[s] of the United States," and their "estate, survivors, or heirs." § 2333(a). In contrast, the ATS is available only for claims brought by "an alien." 28 U.S.C. § 1350. A statute that excludes foreign nationals (with the possible exception of foreign survivors or heirs) is an inapt analogy for a common-law cause of action that provides a remedy for foreign nationals only.

To the extent, furthermore, that the Anti-Terrorism Act is relevant it suggests that there should be no common-law action under the ATS for allegations like petitioners'. Otherwise, foreign plaintiffs could bypass Congress's express limitations on liability under the Anti-Terrorism Act simply by bringing an ATS lawsuit. The Anti-Terrorism Act . . . is part of a comprehensive statutory and regulatory regime that prohibits terrorism and terrorism financing. The detailed regulatory structures prescribed by Congress and the federal agencies charged with oversight of financial institutions reflect the careful deliberation of the political branches on when, and how, banks should be held liable for the financing of terrorism. It would be inappropriate for courts to displace this considered statutory and regulatory structure by holding banks subject to common-law liability in actions filed under the ATS.

In any event, even if the Anti-Terrorism Act were a suitable model for an ATS suit, Congress's decision in the TVPA to limit liability to individuals still demonstrates that there are two reasonable choices. In this area, that is dispositive—Congress, not the Judiciary, must decide whether to expand the scope of liability under the ATS to include foreign corporations.

3

Other considerations relevant to the exercise of judicial discretion also counsel against allowing liability under the ATS for foreign corporations, absent instructions from Congress to do so. It has not been shown that corporate liability under the ATS is essential to serve the goals of the statute. As to the question of adequate remedies, the ATS will seldom be the only way for plaintiffs to hold the perpetrators liable. See, e.g., 18 U.S.C. § 1091 (criminal prohibition on genocide); § 1595 (civil remedy for victims of slavery). And plaintiffs still can sue the individual corporate employees responsible for a violation of international law under the ATS. If the Court were to hold that foreign corporations have liability for international-law violations, then plaintiffs may well ignore the human perpetrators and concentrate instead on multinational corporate entities.

. . . [I]n the context of criminal tribunals international law itself generally limits liability to natural persons. Although the Court need not decide whether the seeming absence of a specific, universal, and obligatory norm of corporate liability under international law by itself forecloses petitioners' claims against Arab Bank, or whether this is an issue governed by international law, the lack of a clear and well-established international-law rule is of critical relevance in determining whether courts should extend ATS liability to foreign corporations without specific congressional authorization to do so. That is especially so in light of the TVPA's limitation of liability to natural persons, which parallels the distinction between corporations and individuals in international law.

If, moreover, the Court were to hold that foreign corporations may be held liable under the ATS, that precedent-setting principle "would imply that other nations, also applying the law of nations, could hale our [corporations] into their courts for alleged violations of the law of nations." *Kiobel*, 569 U.S. at 124. This judicially mandated doctrine, in turn, could subject American corporations to an immediate, constant risk of claims seeking to impose massive liability for the alleged conduct of their employees and subsidiaries around the world, all as determined in foreign courts, thereby "hinder[ing] global investment in developing economies, where it is most needed." Brief for United States as Amicus Curiae in *American Isuzu Motors, Inc. v. Ntsebeza*, O.T. 2007, No. 07–919, p. 20.

In other words, allowing plaintiffs to sue foreign corporations under the ATS could establish a precedent that discourages American corporations from investing abroad, including in developing economies where the host government might have a history of alleged human-rights violations, or where judicial systems might lack the safeguards of United States courts. And, in consequence, that often might deter the active corporate investment that contributes to the economic development that so often is an essential foundation for human rights.

It is also true, of course, that natural persons can and do use corporations for sinister purposes, including conduct that violates international law. That the corporate form can be an instrument for inflicting grave harm and suffering poses serious and complex questions both for the international community and for Congress. So there are strong arguments for permitting the victims to seek relief from corporations themselves. Yet the urgency and complexity of this problem make it all the more important that Congress determine whether victims of human-rights abuses may sue foreign corporations in federal courts in the United States. Congress, not the Judiciary, is the branch with "the facilities necessary to make fairly such an important policy decision where the possibilities of international discord are so evident and retaliative action so certain." *Kiobel*, 569 U.S. at 116. As noted further below, there are many delicate and important considerations that Congress is in a better position to examine in determining whether and how best to impose corporate liability. And, as the TVPA illustrates, Congress is well aware of the necessity of clarifying the proper scope of liability under the ATS in a timely way.

C

The ATS was intended to promote harmony in international relations by ensuring foreign plaintiffs a remedy for international-law violations in circumstances where the absence of such a remedy might provoke foreign nations to hold the United States accountable. Brief for United States as Amicus Curiae 7. But here, and in similar cases, the opposite is occurring.

Petitioners are foreign nationals seeking hundreds of millions of dollars in damages from a major Jordanian financial institution for injuries suffered in attacks by foreign terrorists in the Middle East. The only alleged connections to the United States are [electronic currency clearance] transactions in Arab Bank's New York branch and a brief allegation regarding a charity in Texas. The Court of Appeals did not address, and the Court need not now decide, whether these allegations are sufficient to "touch and concern" the United States under *Kiobel*.

At a minimum, the relatively minor connection between the terrorist attacks at issue in this case and the alleged conduct in the United States well illustrates the perils of extending the scope of ATS liability to foreign multinational corporations like Arab Bank. For 13 years, this litigation has "caused significant diplomatic tensions" with Jordan, a critical ally in one of the world's most sensitive regions. Brief for United States as Amicus Curiae 30. "Jordan is a key counterterrorism partner, especially in the global campaign to defeat the Islamic State in Iraq and Syria." Id. at 31. The United States explains that Arab Bank itself is "a constructive partner with the United States in working to prevent terrorist financing." Id. at 32 (internal quotation marks omitted). Jordan considers the instant litigation to be a "grave affront" to its sovereignty. See Brief for Hashemite Kingdom of Jordan as Amicus Curiae 3.

This is not the first time, furthermore, that a foreign sovereign has appeared in this Court to note its objections to ATS litigation. . . . These are the very foreign-relations tensions the First Congress sought to avoid.

Petitioners insist that whatever the faults of this litigation—for example, its tenuous connections to the United States and the prolonged diplomatic disruptions it has caused—the fact that Arab Bank is a foreign corporate entity, as distinct from a natural person, is not one of them. That misses the point. As demonstrated by this litigation, foreign corporate defendants create unique problems. And courts are not well suited to make the required policy judgments that are implicated by corporate liability in cases like this one.

Like the presumption against extraterritoriality, judicial caution under *Sosa* "guards against our courts triggering . . . serious foreign policy consequences, and instead defers such decisions, quite appropriately, to the political branches." *Kiobel*, 569 U.S. at 124. If, in light of all the concerns that must be weighed before imposing liability on foreign corporations via ATS suits, the Court were to hold that it has the discretion to make that determination, then the cautionary language of *Sosa* would be little more than empty rhetoric. Accordingly, the Court holds that foreign corporations may not be defendants in suits brought under the ATS.

III

With the ATS, the First Congress provided a federal remedy for a narrow category of international-law violations committed by individuals. Whether, more than two centuries on, a similar remedy should be available against foreign corporations is similarly a decision that Congress must make.

The political branches can determine, referring to international law to the extent they deem proper, whether to impose liability for human-rights violations upon foreign corporations in this Nation's courts, and, conversely, that courts in other countries should be able to hold United States corporations liable. Congress might determine that violations of international law do, or should, impose that liability to ensure that corporations make every effort to deter human-rights violations, and so that, even when those efforts cannot be faulted, compensation for injured persons will be a cost of doing business. If Congress and the Executive were to determine that corporations should be liable for violations of international law, that decision would have special power and force because it would be made by the branches most immediately responsive to, and accountable to, the electorate.

It is still another possibility that, in the careful exercise of its expertise in the field of foreign affairs, Congress might conclude that neutral judicial safeguards may not be ensured in every country; and so, as a reciprocal matter, it could determine that liability of foreign corporations under the ATS should be subject to some limitations or preconditions. Congress might deem this more careful course to be the best way to encourage American corporations to undertake the extensive investments and foreign operations that can be an important beginning point for creating the infrastructures that allow human rights, as well as judicial safeguards, to emerge. These delicate judgments, involving a balance that it is the prerogative of the political branches to make, especially in the field of foreign affairs, would, once again, also be entitled to special respect, especially because those careful distinctions might themselves advance the Rule of Law. All this underscores the important separation-of-powers concerns that require the Judiciary to refrain from making these kinds of decisions under the ATS. The political branches, moreover, surely are better positioned than the Judiciary to determine if corporate liability would, or would not, create special risks of disrupting good relations with foreign governments.

Finally, Congress might find that corporate liability should be limited to cases where a corporation's management was actively complicit in the crime. Cf. ALI, Model Penal Code § 2.07(1)(c) (1985) (a corporation may be held criminally liable where "the commission of the offense was authorized, requested, commanded, performed or recklessly tolerated by the board of directors or by a high managerial agent acting on behalf of the corporation within the scope of his office or employment"). Again, the political branches are better equipped to make the preliminary findings and consequent conclusions that should inform this determination.

These and other considerations that must shape and instruct the formulation of principles of international and domestic law are matters that the political branches are in the better position to define and articulate. For these reasons, judicial deference requires that any imposition of corporate liability on foreign corporations for violations of international law must be determined in the first instance by the political branches of the Government.

The judgment of the Court of Appeals is affirmed.

It is so ordered.

■ JUSTICE THOMAS, concurring.

I join the Court's opinion in full because it correctly applies our precedents. I also agree with the points raised by my concurring colleagues. Courts should not be in the business of creating new causes of action under the Alien Tort Statute (Gorsuch, J., concurring in part and concurring in judgment), especially when it risks international strife (Alito, J., concurring in part and concurring in judgment). And the Alien Tort Statute likely does not apply to suits between foreign plaintiffs and foreign defendants (opinion of Gorsuch, J.).

■ JUSTICE ALITO, concurring in part and concurring in the judgment.

Creating causes of action under the Alien Tort Statute against foreign corporate defendants would precipitate exactly the sort of diplomatic strife that the law was enacted to prevent. As a result, I agree with the Court that we should not take that step, and I join Parts I, II-B-1, and II-C of the opinion of the Court. I write separately to elaborate on why that outcome is compelled not only by "judicial caution," but also by the separation of powers. . . .

For the reasons articulated by Justice Scalia in Sosa v. Alvarez-Machain, 542 U.S. 692 (2004), and by Justice Gorsuch today, I am not certain that *Sosa* was correctly decided. But even taking that decision on its own terms, this Court should not create causes of action under the ATS against foreign corporate defendants. As part of *Sosa*'s second step, a court should decline to create a cause of action as a matter of federal common law where the result would be to further, not avoid, diplomatic strife. Properly applied, that rule easily resolves the question presented by this case.*

Sosa interpreted the ATS to authorize the federal courts to create causes of action as a matter of federal common law. We have repeatedly emphasized that "in fashioning federal [common law] principles to govern areas left open by Congress, our function is to effectuate congressional policy." United States v. Kimbell Foods, Inc., 440 U.S. 715, 738 (1979). Fidelity to congressional policy is not only prudent but necessary: Going beyond the bounds of Congress's authorization would mean unconstitutionally usurping part of the "legislative Powers." U.S. Const., Art. I, § 1. Accordingly, the objective for courts in every case requiring the creation of federal common law must be "to find the rule that will best effectuate the federal policy." Textile Workers v. Lincoln Mills of Ala., 353 U.S. 448, 457 (1957).

The ATS was meant to help the United States avoid diplomatic friction. The First Congress enacted the law to provide a forum for adjudicating that "narrow set of violations of the law of nations" that, if left unaddressed, "threaten[ed] serious consequences" for the United States. *Sosa*, 542 U.S. at 715. Specifically, the First Congress was concerned about offenses like piracy, violation of safe conducts, and infringement of the rights of ambassadors, each of which "if not adequately redressed could rise to an issue of war." Id. That threat was existentially terrifying for the young Nation. To minimize the danger, the First Congress enacted the ATS, "ensur[ing] that the United States could provide a forum for adjudicating such incidents" and thus helping the Nation avoid further diplomatic imbroglios. Kiobel v. Royal Dutch Petroleum Co., 569 U.S. 108, 114, 124 (2013).

Putting that objective together with the rules governing federal common law generally, the following principle emerges: Federal courts should decline to create federal common law causes of action under *Sosa*'s second step whenever doing so would not materially advance the ATS's objective of avoiding diplomatic strife. And applying that principle here, it is clear that federal courts should not create causes of action under the

---

* Because this case involves a foreign corporation, we have no need to reach the question whether an alien may sue a United States corporation under the ATS. And since such a suit may generally be brought in federal court based on diversity jurisdiction, 28 U.S.C. § 1332(a)(2), it is unclear why ATS jurisdiction would be needed in that situation.

ATS against foreign corporate defendants. All parties agree that customary international law does not *require* corporate liability as a general matter. But if customary international law does not require corporate liability, then declining to create it under the ATS cannot give other nations just cause for complaint against the United States.

To the contrary, ATS suits against foreign corporations may provoke—and, indeed, frequently *have* provoked—exactly the sort of diplomatic strife inimical to the fundamental purpose of the ATS. Some foreign states appear to interpret international law as foreclosing civil corporate liability for violations of the law of nations. Creating ATS causes of action against foreign corporate defendants would put the United States at odds with these nations. Even when states do not object to this sort of corporate liability as a *legal* matter, they may be concerned about ATS suits against their corporations for political reasons. For example, Jordan considers this suit "a direct affront" to its sovereignty and one that "risks destabilizing Jordan's economy and undercutting one of the most stable and productive alliances the United States has in the Middle East." Brief for Hashemite Kingdom of Jordan as Amicus Curiae 4. Courting these sorts of problems—which seem endemic to ATS litigation—was the opposite of what the First Congress had in mind.

In response, the dissent argues merely that any diplomatic friction "can be addressed with a tool more tailored to the source of the problem than a blanket ban on corporate liability." Even on its own terms, that argument is problematic: Many of the "more tailored" tools offered by the dissent will still be hotly litigated by ATS plaintiffs, and it may be years before incorrect initial decisions about their applicability can be reviewed by the courts of appeals.

In any event, the dissent misunderstands the relevant standard. The question before us is whether the United States would be embroiled in fewer international controversies if we created causes of action under the ATS against foreign corporate defendants. Unless corporate liability would actively *decrease* diplomatic disputes, we have no authority to act. On that score, the dissent can only speculate that declining to create causes of action against foreign corporate defendants "might" lead to diplomatic friction. But the dissent has no real-world examples to support its hunch, and that is not surprising; the ATS already goes further than any other statute in the world in granting aliens the right to sue civilly for violations of international law, especially in light of the many other avenues for relief available. It would be rather rich for any other nation to complain that the ATS does not go far enough. Indeed, no country has. . . .

Creating causes of action under the ATS against foreign corporate defendants would be a no-win proposition. Foreign corporate liability would not only fail to meaningfully advance the objectives of the ATS, but it would also lead to precisely those "serious consequences in international affairs" that the ATS was enacted to avoid. *Sosa*, 542 U. S. at

715. Under those circumstances, federal courts have a duty to refrain from acting. Although that may make it more difficult for aliens to hold foreign corporations liable for human rights abuses, we have repeatedly rejected the view that the ATS was meant to transform the federal courts into forums for the litigation of all human rights suits. Declining to extend the ATS to foreign corporate defendants is thus not about "[i]mmunizing corporations that violate human rights," but rather about furthering the purpose that the ATS was actually meant to serve—avoiding diplomatic strife.

■ JUSTICE GORSUCH, concurring in part and concurring in the judgment.

I am pleased to join the Court's judgment and Parts I, II-B-1, and II-C of its opinion. Respectfully, though, I believe there are two more fundamental reasons why this lawsuit must be dismissed. A group of foreign plaintiffs wants a federal court to invent a new cause of action so they can sue another foreigner for allegedly breaching international norms. In any other context, a federal judge faced with a request like that would know exactly what to do with it: dismiss it out of hand. Not because the defendant happens to be a corporation instead of a human being. But because the job of creating new causes of action and navigating foreign policy disputes belongs to the political branches. For reasons passing understanding, federal courts have sometimes treated the Alien Tort Statute as a license to overlook these foundational principles. I would end ATS exceptionalism. We should refuse invitations to create new forms of legal liability. And we should not meddle in disputes between foreign citizens over international norms. I write because I am hopeful that courts in the future might pause to consider both of these reasons for restraint before taking up cases like this one. Whatever powers courts may possess in ATS suits, they are powers judges should be doubly careful not to abuse.

First adopted in 1789, the current version of the ATS provides that "[t]he district courts shall have original jurisdiction of any civil action by an alien for a tort only, committed in violation of the law of nations or a treaty of the United States." 28 U.S.C. § 1350. More than two hundred years later, the meaning of this terse provision has still "proven elusive." Sosa v. Alvarez-Machain, 542 U.S. 692, 719 (2004). At the same time, this Court has suggested that Congress enacted the statute to afford federal courts jurisdiction to hear tort claims related to three violations of international law that were already embodied in English common law: violations of safe conducts extended to aliens, interference with ambassadors, and piracy. Id. at 715; 4 W. Blackstone, Commentaries on the Laws of England 68 (1769) (Blackstone); see also Anthony J. Bellia, Jr. & Bradford R. Clark, The Alien Tort Statute and the Law of Nations, 78 U. Chi. L. Rev. 445 (2011) (arguing that the ATS meant to supply jurisdiction over a slightly larger set of claims involving intentional torts by Americans against aliens).

In this case, the plaintiffs seek much more. They want the federal courts to recognize a new cause of action, one that did not exist at the time of the statute's adoption, one that Congress has never authorized. While their request might appear inconsistent with *Sosa*'s explanation of the ATS's modest origin, the plaintiffs say that a caveat later in the opinion saves them. They point to a passage where the Court went on to suggest that the ATS may *also* afford federal judges "discretion [to] conside[r] [creating] new cause[s] of action" if they "rest on a norm of international character accepted by the civilized world and defined with a specificity comparable to the features of the [three] 18th-century" torts the Court already described. *Sosa*, 542 U.S. at 725.

I harbor serious doubts about *Sosa*'s suggestion. In our democracy the people's elected representatives make the laws that govern them. Judges do not. . . . Adopting new causes of action may have been a "proper function for common-law courts," but it is not appropriate "for federal tribunals" mindful of the limits of their constitutional authority. Alexander v. Sandoval, 532 U.S. 275, 287 (2001).

Nor can I see any reason to make a special exception for the ATS. As *Sosa* initially acknowledged, the ATS was designed as "a jurisdictional statute creating no new causes of action." 542 U.S. at 724. And I would have thought that the end of the matter. A statute that creates no new causes of action . . . creates no new causes of action. To the extent *Sosa* continued on to claim for federal judges the discretionary power to create new forms of liability on their own, it invaded terrain that belongs to the people's representatives and should be promptly returned to them.

But even accepting *Sosa*'s framework does not end the matter. As the Court acknowledges, there is a strong argument that "a proper application of *Sosa* would preclude courts from ever recognizing any new causes of action under the ATS." I believe that argument is correct. For the reasons just described, separation of powers considerations ordinarily require us to defer to Congress in the creation of new forms of liability. This Court hasn't yet used *Sosa*'s assertion of discretionary authority to recognize a new cause of action, and I cannot imagine a sound reason, hundreds of years after the statute's passage, to start now. For a court inclined to claim the discretion to enter this field, it is a discretion best exercised by staying out of it. . . .

Another independent problem lurks here. This is a suit by foreigners against a foreigner over the meaning of international norms. Respectfully, I do not think the original understanding of the ATS or our precedent permits federal courts to hear cases like this. At a minimum, both those considerations and simple common sense about the limits of the judicial function should lead federal courts to require a domestic defendant before agreeing to exercise any *Sosa*-generated discretion to entertain an ATS suit.

Start with the statute. What we call the Alien Tort Statute began as just one clause among many in § 9 of the Judiciary Act of 1789, which specified the jurisdiction of the federal courts. 1 Stat. 76–78. . . . Like today's recodified version, 28 U.S.C. § 1350, the original text of the ATS did not expressly call for a U.S. defendant. But I think it likely would have been understood to contain such a requirement when adopted.

That is because the First Congress passed the Judiciary Act in the shadow of the Constitution. The Act created the federal courts and vested them with statutory authority to entertain claims consistent with the newly ratified terms of Article III. Meanwhile, under Article III, Congress could not have extended to federal courts the power to hear just any suit between two aliens (unless, for example, one was a diplomat). Diversity of citizenship was required. So, because Article III's diversity-of-citizenship clause calls for a U.S. party, and because the ATS clause requires an alien plaintiff, it follows that an American defendant was needed for an ATS suit to proceed.

Precedent confirms this conclusion. In Mossman v. Higginson, 4 U.S. 12, 14 (1800), this Court addressed the meaning of a neighboring provision of the Judiciary Act. Section 11 gave the circuit courts power to hear, among other things, civil cases where "an alien is a party." 1 Stat. 78. As with § 9, you might think § 11's language could be read to permit a suit *between* aliens. Yet this Court held § 11 must instead be construed to refer only to cases "where, indeed, an alien is one party, but a citizen is the other." *Mossman*, 4 Dall. at 14 (internal quotation marks omitted). That was necessary, *Mossman* explained, to give the statute a "constructio[n] consistent" with the diversity-jurisdiction clause of Article III. And as a matter of precedent, I cannot think of a good reason why we would now read § 9 differently than *Mossman* read § 11. . . .

Nor does it appear the ATS meant to rely on any other head of Article III jurisdiction. You might wonder, for example, if the First Congress considered a "violation of the law of nations" to be a violation of, and thus "arise under," federal law. But that does not seem likely. . . . While this Court has called international law "part of our law," The Paquete Habana, 175 U.S. 677, 700 (1900), and a component of the "law of the land," The Nereide, 13 U.S. 388 (1815), that simply meant international law was no different than the law of torts or contracts—it was "part of the so-called general common law," but *not* part of federal law. *Sosa*, 542 U.S. at 739–40 (opinion of Scalia, J.). See Curtis A. Bradley & Jack L. Goldsmith, Customary International Law as Federal Common Law: A Critique of the Modern Position, 110 Harv. L. Rev. 815, 824, 849–50 (1997); see also Ernest A. Young, Sorting Out the Debate Over Customary International Law, 42 Va. J. Int'l L. 365, 374–75 (2002). . . .

Any attempt to decipher a cryptic old statute is sure to meet with challenges. For example, one could object that this reading of the Act does not assign to the ATS the work of addressing assaults by aliens against foreign ambassadors on our soil, even though *Sosa* suggested the statute was enacted partly in response to precisely such a case: the "Marbois incident of May 1784, in which a French adventurer, De Longchamps, verbally and physically assaulted the Secretary of the French Legion in Philadelphia." 542 U.S. at 716. Many thought that the States' failure to provide a forum for relief to the foreign minister was a scandal and part of what prompted the framers of the Constitution to strengthen the national government.

But worries along these lines may be misplaced. The ATS was never meant to serve as a freestanding statute, only as one clause in one section of the Judiciary Act. So even if you think *something* in the Judiciary Act must be interpreted to address the Marbois incident, that doesn't mean it must be the ATS clause. And, as it happens, a different provision of the Act *did* deal expressly with the problem of ambassadorial assaults: Section 13 conferred on this Court "original, but not exclusive jurisdiction of all suits brought by ambassadors, or other public ministers, or in which a consul, or vice consul shall be a party." 1 Stat. 80–81. That implemented Article III's provision empowering us to hear suits "affecting Ambassadors, other public ministers and Consuls." § 2. And given that § 13 deals with the problem of "ambassadors" so directly, it is unclear why we must read § 9 to address that same problem. See Thomas H. Lee, The Safe-Conduct Theory of the Alien Tort Statute, 106 Colum. L. Rev. 830, 855–58 (2006).

Along different but similar lines, some might be concerned that requiring a U.S. defendant in ATS suits would leave the problem of piracy inadequately addressed, given that *Sosa* suggested that piracy was one of the three offenses the ATS may have meant to capture, and many pirates were foreigners. But here the response is much the same. A separate clause of § 9 gave the district courts "exclusive original cognizance of all civil causes of admiralty and maritime jurisdiction." 1 Stat. 77. That statute has long been given a broad construction covering "all maritime contracts, torts and injuries," DeLovio v. Boit, 7 F. Cas. 418, 442 (No. 3,776) (CC Mass. 1815) (Story, J.), along with "prize jurisdiction, which probably included almost all 'piracy' cases after 1789," Lee, supra, at 867. So it is not clear why it's necessary to cram the problem of piracy into the ATS. If anything, it may be necessary *not* to do so. . . .

If doubt lingers on these historical questions, it is a doubt that should counsel restraint all the same. Even if the ATS might have meant to allow foreign *ambassadors* to sue foreign defendants, or foreign plaintiffs to sue foreign *pirates*, what would that prove about more mine-run cases like ours, where none of those special concerns are implicated? There are at least serious historical arguments suggesting the ATS was not meant to apply to suits like this one. And to the extent *Sosa* affords courts discretion to proceed, these arguments should inform any decision whether to exercise that discretion. . . .

Any consideration of *Sosa*'s discretion must also account for proper limits on the judicial function. As discussed above, federal courts generally lack the institutional expertise and constitutional authority to oversee foreign policy and national security, and should be wary of straying where they do not belong. Yet there are degrees of institutional incompetence and constitutional evil. It is one thing for courts to assume the task of creating new causes of action to ensure *our* citizens abide by the law of nations and *avoid* reprisals against this country. It is altogether another thing for courts to punish *foreign* parties for conduct that could not be attributed to the United States and thereby *risk* reprisals against this country. If a foreign state or citizen violates an "international norm" in a way that offends another foreign state or citizen, the Constitution arms the President and Congress with ample means to address it. Or, if they think best, the political branches may choose to look the other way. But in all events, the decision to impose sanctions in disputes between foreigners over international norms is not ours to make. It is a decision that belongs to those answerable to the people and assigned by the Constitution to defend this nation. If they wish our help, they are free to enlist it, but we should not ever be in the business of elbowing our way in.

▪ JUSTICE SOTOMAYOR, with whom JUSTICE GINSBURG, JUSTICE BREYER, and JUSTICE KAGAN join, dissenting.

The Court today holds that the Alien Tort Statute (ATS), 28 U.S.C. § 1350, categorically forecloses foreign corporate liability. In so doing, it absolves corporations from responsibility under the ATS for conscience-shocking behavior. I disagree both with the Court's conclusion and its analytic approach. The text, history, and purpose of the ATS, as well as the long and consistent history of corporate liability in tort, confirm that tort claims for law-of-nations violations may be brought against corporations under the ATS. Nothing about the corporate form in itself raises foreign-policy concerns that require the Court, as a matter of common-law discretion, to immunize all foreign corporations from liability under the ATS, regardless of the specific law-of-nations violations alleged. I respectfully dissent. . . .

The plurality assumes without deciding that whether corporations can be permissible defendants under the ATS turns on the first step of the two-part inquiry set out in Sosa v. Alvarez-Machain, 542 U.S. 692 (2004). But by asking whether there is "a specific, universal, and obligatory norm of liability for corporations" in international law, the plurality fundamentally misconceives how international law works and so misapplies the first step of *Sosa*. . . .

Sosa's norm-specific first step is inapposite to the categorical question whether corporations may be sued under the ATS as a general matter. International law imposes certain obligations that are intended to govern the behavior of states and private actors. Among those obligations are substantive prohibitions on certain conduct thought to violate human rights, such as genocide, slavery, extrajudicial killing, and torture. Substantive prohibitions like these are the norms at which *Sosa*'s step-one inquiry is aimed and for which *Sosa* requires that there be sufficient international consensus.

Sosa does not, however, demand that there be sufficient international consensus with regard to the mechanisms of enforcing these norms, for enforcement is not a question with which customary international law is concerned. Although international law determines what substantive conduct violates the law of nations, it leaves the specific rules of how to enforce international-law norms and remedy their violation to states, which may act to impose liability collectively through treaties or independently via their domestic legal systems. . . .

Instead of asking whether there exists a specific, universal, and obligatory norm of corporate liability under international law, the relevant inquiry in response to the question presented here is whether there is any reason—under either international law or our domestic law—to distinguish between a corporation and a natural person who is alleged to have violated the law of nations under the ATS. . . . The text, history, and purpose of the ATS plainly support the conclusion that corporations may be held liable.

Beginning "with the language of the statute itself," United States v. Ron Pair Enterprises, Inc., 489 U.S. 235, 241 (1989), two aspects of the text of the ATS make clear that the statute allows corporate liability. First, the text confers jurisdiction on federal district courts to hear "civil action[s]" for "tort[s]." 28 U.S.C. § 1350. Where Congress uses a term of art like tort, "it presumably knows and adopts the cluster of ideas that were attached to [the] borrowed word in the body of learning from which it was taken and the meaning its use will convey to the judicial mind unless otherwise instructed." Morissette v. United States, 342 U.S. 246, 263 (1952).

Corporations have long been held liable in tort under the federal common law. This Court "has assumed that, when Congress creates a tort action, it legislates against a legal background of ordinary tort-related . . . rules and consequently intends its legislation to incorporate those rules." Meyer v. Holley, 537 U.S. 280, 285 (2003). The presumption, then, is that, in providing for "tort" liability, the ATS provides for corporate liability.

Second, whereas the ATS expressly limits the class of permissible plaintiffs to "alien[s]," § 1350, it "does not distinguish among classes of defendants," Argentine Republic v. Amerada Hess Shipping Corp., 488 U.S. 428, 438 (1989). That silence as to defendants cannot be presumed to be inadvertent. That is because in the same section of the Judiciary Act of 1789 as what is now the ATS, Congress provided the federal district courts with jurisdiction over "all suits against consuls or vice-consuls." § 9, 1 Stat. 76–77. Where Congress wanted to limit the range of permissible defendants, then, it clearly knew how to do so.

Nothing about the historical background against which the ATS was enacted rebuts the presumption that the statute incorporated the accepted principle of corporate liability for tortious conduct. Under the Articles of Confederation, the Continental Congress was unable to provide redress to foreign citizens for violations of treaties or the law of nations, which threatened to undermine the United States' relationships with other nations. The First Congress responded with, *inter alia*, the ATS. Although the two incidents that highlighted the need to provide foreign citizens with a federal forum in which to pursue their grievances involved conflicts between natural persons, . . . there is "no reason to conclude that the First Congress was supremely concerned with the risk that natural persons would cause the United States to be drawn into foreign entanglements, but was content to allow formal legal associations of individuals, i.e., corporations, to do so," Doe v. Exxon Mobil Corp., 654 F.3d 11, 47 (D.C. Cir. 2011), vacated on other grounds, 527 Fed. Appx. 7 (D.C. Cir. 2013). Indeed, foreclosing corporations from liability under the ATS would have been at odds with the contemporaneous practice of imposing liability for piracy on ships, juridical entities. . . .

[Justice Gorsuch's] concurrence suggests that federal courts may lack jurisdiction to entertain suits between aliens based solely on a violation of the law of nations. It contends that ATS suits between aliens fall under neither the federal courts' diversity jurisdiction nor our federal question jurisdiction. The Court was not unaware of this argument when it decided *Sosa*. . . . The Court nonetheless proceeded to decide the case, which it could not have done had it been concerned about its Article III power to do so. That decision forecloses the argument the concurrence now makes, as *Sosa* authorized courts to "recognize private claims *under federal common law* for violations of" certain international law norms. 542 U.S. at 732 (emphasis added).

Sosa was correct as a legal matter. Moreover, our Nation has an interest not only in providing a remedy when our own citizens commit law of nations violations, but also in preventing our Nation from serving as a safe harbor for today's pirates. . . . To the extent suits against foreign defendants may lead to international friction, that concern is better addressed under the presumption the Court established in *Kiobel* against extraterritorial application of the ATS than it is by relitigating settled precedent.

. . . Nothing about the corporate form in itself justifies categorically foreclosing corporate liability in all ATS actions. Each source of diplomatic friction that respondent Arab Bank and the plurality identify can be addressed with a tool more tailored to the source of the problem than a blanket ban on corporate liability.

Arab Bank contends that foreign citizens should not be able "to sue a Jordanian corporation in New York for events taking place in the Middle East." Brief for Respondent 42. The heart of that qualm was already addressed in *Kiobel*, which held that the presumption against extraterritoriality applies to the ATS. . . .

Arab Bank also bemoans the unfairness of being sued when others—namely, the individuals and organizations that carried out the terrorist attacks—were "the direct cause" of the harm petitioners here suffered.

Brief for Respondent 41. That complaint, though, is a critique of the imposition of liability for financing terrorism, not an argument that ATS suits against corporations generally necessarily cause diplomatic tensions.

Arab Bank further expresses concern that ATS suits are being filed against corporations in an effort to recover for the bad acts of foreign governments or officials. But the Bank's explanation of this problem reveals that the true source of its grievance is the availability of aiding and abetting liability.... Yet not all law-of-nations violations asserted against corporations are premised on aiding and abetting liability; it is possible for a corporation to violate international-law norms independent of a foreign state or foreign state officials. In this respect, too, the Court's rule is ill fitted to the problem identified.

Notably, even the Hashemite Kingdom of Jordan does not argue that there are foreign-policy tensions inherent in suing a corporation generally. Instead, Jordan contends that this particular suit is an affront to its sovereignty because of its extraterritorial character and because of the role that Arab Bank specifically plays in the Jordanian economy.

The majority also cites to instances in which other foreign sovereigns have "appeared in this Court to note [their] objections to ATS litigation," but none of those objections was about the availability of corporate liability as a general matter.

As the United States urged at oral argument, when international friction arises, a court should respond with the doctrine that speaks directly to the friction's source. In addition to the presumption against extraterritoriality, federal courts have at their disposal a number of tools to address any foreign-relations concerns that an ATS case may raise. This Court has held that a federal court may exercise personal jurisdiction over a foreign corporate defendant only if the corporation is incorporated in the United States, has its principal place of business or is otherwise at home here, or if the activities giving rise to the lawsuit occurred or had their impact here. See Daimler AG v. Bauman, 571 U.S. 117 (2014). Courts also can dismiss ATS suits for a plaintiff's failure to exhaust the remedies available in her domestic forum, on forum non conveniens grounds, for reasons of international comity, or when asked to do so by the State Department.

Several of these doctrines might be implicated in this case, and I would remand for the Second Circuit to address them in the first instance. The majority, however, prefers to use a sledgehammer to crack a nut. I see no need for such an ill-fitting and disproportionate response. Foreclosing foreign corporate liability in all ATS actions, irrespective of circumstance or norm, is simply too broad a response to case-specific concerns that can be addressed via other means....

The plurality extrapolates from Congress's decision regarding the scope of liability under the TVPA a rule that it contends should govern all ATS suits. But there is no reason to think that because Congress saw fit to permit suits only against natural persons for two specific law-of-nations violations, Congress meant to foreclose corporate liability for all law-of-nations violations. . . .

To infer from the TVPA that no corporation may ever be held liable under the ATS for any violation of any international-law norm, moreover, ignores that Congress has elsewhere imposed liability on corporations for conduct prohibited by customary international law. For instance, the Antiterrorism Act of 1990 (ATA) created a civil cause of action for U.S. nationals injured by an act of international terrorism and expressly provides for corporate liability. 18 U.S.C. § 2333. That Congress foreclosed corporate liability for torture and extrajudicial killing claims under the TVPA but permitted corporate liability for terrorism-related claims under the ATA is strong evidence that Congress exercises its judgment as to the appropriateness of corporate liability on a norm-by-norm basis, and that courts should do the same when considering whether to permit causes of action against corporations for law-of-nations violations under the ATS. . . .

Moreover, even if there are other grounds on which a suit alleging conduct constituting a law-of-nations violation can be brought, such as a state-law tort claim, the First Congress created the ATS because it wanted foreign plaintiffs to be able to bring their claims in federal court and sue for law-of-nations violations. A suit for state-law battery, even if based on the same alleged conduct, is not the equivalent of a federal suit for torture; the latter contributes to the uptake of international human rights norms, and the former does not.

Furthermore, holding corporations accountable for violating the human rights of foreign citizens when those violations touch and concern the United States may well be necessary to avoid the international tension with which the First Congress was concerned. Consider again the assault on the Secretary of the French Legation in Philadelphia by a French adventurer. Would the diplomatic strife that followed really have been any less charged if a corporation had sent its agent to accost the Secretary? Or, consider piracy. If a corporation owned a fleet of vessels and directed them to seize other ships in U.S. waters, there no doubt would be calls to hold the corporation to account. Finally, take, for example, a corporation posing as a job-placement agency that actually traffics in persons, forcibly transporting foreign nationals to the United States for exploitation and profiting from their abuse. Not only are the individual employees of that business less likely to be able fully to compensate successful ATS plaintiffs, but holding only individual employees liable does not impose accountability for the institution-wide disregard for human rights. Absent a corporate sanction, that harm will persist unremedied. Immunizing the corporation from suit under the ATS merely because it is a corporation, even though the violations stemmed directly from corporate policy and practice, might cause serious diplomatic friction. . . .

In categorically barring all suits against foreign corporations under the ATS, the Court ensures that foreign corporations—entities capable of wrongdoing under our domestic law—remain immune from liability for human rights abuses, however egregious they may be. . . .

Immunizing corporations that violate human rights from liability under the ATS undermines the system of accountability for law-of-nations violations that the First Congress endeavored to impose. It allows these entities to take advantage of the significant benefits of the corporate form and enjoy fundamental rights, without having to shoulder attendant fundamental responsibilities.

I respectfully dissent.

NOTES ON JESNER V. ARAB BANK

1. CORPORATE ATS LIABILITY

Since the 1990s, numerous ATS suits have been brought against private corporations on the theory that the corporations either have violated one of the few international human rights norms that apply to private actors (such as the prohibition on slavery) or that the corporations have "aided and abetted" violations of international human rights law committed by foreign governments. The allegations in these cases have varied, ranging from claims that corporations were merely doing business with oppressive regimes to claims that the corporations were knowingly participating in abuses. The lower courts generally assumed in such cases that corporations could be sued, although there was substantial debate over the proper standards for liability.

In Kiobel v. Royal Dutch Petroleum Co., 621 F.3d 111 (2d Cir. 2010), the Second Circuit held that ATS suits could not be brought against private corporations. The court reasoned that, in order for a defendant's conduct to be actionable under the ATS, the conduct must violate international law, and it concluded that international human rights law did not extend to conduct by corporations. This decision created a conflict in the circuits. The Supreme Court granted certiorari to resolve the conflict, but, as discussed in the next Note, it ultimately decided the case on other grounds. In the meantime, other circuit courts continued to disagree with the Second Circuit.

As noted earlier in this section, in 1992 Congress enacted the Torture Victim Protection Act (TVPA), which creates a cause of action for claims of torture and "extrajudicial killing" under color of foreign law. The TVPA, which is codified as a note to the ATS, refers to claims by an "individual" against another "individual." Because of this language, the Court held in Mohamad v. Palestinian Authority, 566 U.S. 449 (2012), that the TVPA authorizes suit only against natural persons. The Court observed that, because the ATS does not use the term "individual," it "offers no comparative value here regardless of whether corporate entities can be held liable in a federal common-law action brought under that statute."

2. KIOBEL AND THE PRESUMPTION AGAINST EXTRATERRITORIALITY

The Supreme Court ordinarily presumes that federal statutes apply only to conduct occurring inside the United States. In EEOC v. Arabian American Oil Co., 499 U.S. 244 (1991), the Court applied this "presumption against extraterritoriality" in holding that Title VII of the Civil Rights Act did not apply to a U.S. corporation's alleged discriminatory treatment of a U.S. citizen in Saudi Arabia. In Morrison v. National Australia Bank Ltd., 561 U.S. 247 (2010), the Court applied the presumption in holding that Section 10(b) of the Securities Exchange Act did not apply to claims of alleged misconduct in connection with securities traded on foreign exchanges. The Court explained that the presumption "rests on the perception that Congress ordinarily legislates with respect to domestic, not foreign matters," *Morrison*, 561 U.S. at 255, and that it also "serves to protect against unintended clashes between our laws and those of other nations which could result in international discord," *Arabian American Oil*, 499 U.S. at 248.

Despite the presumption against extraterritoriality, most lower courts prior to 2013 assumed that claims could be brought under the ATS for foreign conduct. One reason they may have made this assumption is that the ATS is limited to torts that violate international law. Since international law applies globally, it may not seem "extraterritorial" for a U.S. court to apply it to adjudicate a dispute concerning conduct abroad.

In Kiobel v. Royal Dutch Petroleum Co., 569 U.S. 108 (2013), however, the Supreme Court "conclude[d] that the presumption against extraterritoriality applies to claims under the ATS, and that nothing in the statute rebuts that presumption." In that case, a group of Nigerian citizens residing in the United States had filed an ATS action in federal court against various non-U.S. corporations, alleging that the corporations had aided and abetted the Nigerian government in committing human rights violations in Nigeria. While the Court acknowledged that it had typically applied the presumption only to statutes that directly regulate conduct, whereas the ATS is a jurisdictional statute that "allows federal courts to recognize certain causes of action," it reasoned that "the principles underlying the canon of interpretation similarly constrain courts considering causes of action that may be brought under the ATS." If anything, said the Court, "the danger of unwarranted judicial interference in the conduct of foreign policy is magnified in the context of the ATS, because the question is not what Congress has done but instead what courts may do."

The Court then proceeded to examine the text, history, and purposes of the ATS, and it concluded that they did not suggest that Congress intended for extraterritorial application of the statute. Among other things, the Court reasoned that there was nothing in the historical context of the ATS that "suggests that Congress . . . intended federal common law under the ATS to provide a cause of action for conduct occurring in the territory of another sovereign." As a result, the Court affirmed the dismissal of this case:

On these facts, all the relevant conduct took place outside the United States. And even where the claims touch and concern the territory of the United States, they must do so with sufficient force to displace the presumption against extraterritorial application. . . . Corporations are often present in many countries, and it would reach too far to say that mere corporate presence suffices. If Congress were to determine otherwise, a statute more specific than the ATS would be required.

Justice Kennedy observed in a short concurrence that the decision left open "significant questions regarding the reach and interpretation of the Alien Tort Statute" and that "the presumption against extraterritorial application may require some further elaboration and explanation" in cases covered "neither by the TVPA nor by the reasoning and holding of today's case." In a separate concurrence, Justice Alito, joined by Justice Thomas, expressed the view that "a putative ATS cause of action will fall within the scope of the presumption against extraterritoriality—and will therefore be barred—unless the domestic conduct is sufficient to violate an international law norm that satisfies [the] requirements [in Sosa v. Alvarez-Machain, 542 U.S. 692 (2004)] of definiteness and acceptance among civilized nations."

Justice Breyer, writing for himself and Justices Ginsburg, Sotomayor, and Kagan, concurred in the judgment upholding dismissal of the case but disagreed with the majority's reasoning. Instead of applying a presumption against extraterritoriality to the ATS, Breyer argued that ATS suits should be allowed in three situations: "where (1) the alleged tort occurs on American soil, (2) the defendant is an American national, or (3) the defendant's conduct substantially and adversely affects an important American national interest, and that includes a distinct interest in preventing the United States from becoming a safe harbor (free of civil as well as criminal liability) for a torturer or other common enemy of mankind." He agreed with the majority, however, that in this case "the parties and relevant conduct lack sufficient ties to the United States for the ATS to provide jurisdiction."

Kiobel imposed a substantial territorial limitation on ATS litigation. There was debate, however, over how broadly to construe this limitation. In particular, there has been disagreement over what must be shown in order to establish that a plaintiff's claims "touch and concern the territory of the United States." If all of the defendant's activities connected to the case occurred abroad, then presumably the "touch and concern" test is not met. Less clear, however, are situations in which it is alleged that the defendant has engaged in conduct in the United States that has helped to facilitate foreign tortious conduct. It was not clear, for example, whether the plaintiffs' claims in *Jesner v. Arab Bank* (which included allegations that electronic transactions were channeled by the defendant bank through its New York City offices) met the "touch and concern" test. The Court in *Jesner* declined to resolve that issue.

3. QUESTIONS AND COMMENTS ON *JESNER V. ARAB BANK*

After *Kiobel* and *Jesne*r, what suits can be brought under the ATS? *Kiobel* disallows many ATS suits involving foreign conduct, and *Jesner* disallows ATS suits against foreign corporations. Do these limitations reflect sensible interpretations of the ATS? In imposing these limitations, the Court has emphasized separation-of-powers considerations. Justice Alito gave even greater emphasis to such considerations in his concurrence in *Jesner*. To what extent are these considerations similar to the ones reflected in the Court's decisions on the other topics covered in this chapter—federal common law, implied statutory rights of action, and *Bivens* remedies? Is the decision in *Jesner* best viewed as leaving an important policy question to be decided by Congress in the first instance, as the majority maintains, or as immunizing corporations from the reach of a generally-worded statute, as the dissent maintains? Note that the Court does not resolve whether *U.S.* corporations may be sued under the ATS. Does its analysis nevertheless suggest an answer to that question?

In his concurrence, Justice Gorsuch suggests that the ATS may have been intended to be limited to cases involving U.S.-citizen defendants. Such an interpretation would provide an easy answer to the question of how ATS suits fall within the Article III jurisdiction of the federal courts: they would fall within Article III "alienage diversity" jurisdiction. Given prior precedents, is it too late for the Court to adopt such an interpretation? For academic commentary supporting this diversity interpretation of the ATS, see Curtis A. Bradley, The Alien Tort Statute and Article III, 42 Va. J. Int'l L. 587 (2002), and Anthony J. Bellia Jr. & Bradford R. Clark, The Alien Tort Statute and the Law of Nations, 78 U. Chi. L. Rev. 445 (2011). For a critique of such an interpretation, see William S. Dodge, The Constitutionality of the Alien Tort Statute: Some Observations on Text and Context, 42 Va. J. Int'l L. 687 (2002).

4. BIBLIOGRAPHY

For discussions of corporate liability under the ATS prior to *Jesner*, see Curtis A. Bradley, State Action and Corporate Human Rights Liability, 85 Notre Dame L. Rev. 1823 (2010); Doug Cassel, Corporate Aiding and Abetting of Human Rights Violations: Confusion in the Courts, 6 Nw. U. J. Int'l Hum. Rts. 304 (2008); Chimene Keitner, Conceptualizing Complicity in Alien Tort Cases, 60 Hastings L.J. 61 (2008); Julian G. Ku, The Curious Case of Corporate Liability Under the Alien Tort Statute: A Flawed System of Judicial Lawmaking, 51 Va. J. Int'l L. 353 (2011); Michael D. Ramsey, International Law Limits on Investor Liability in Human Rights Litigation, 50 Harv. Int'l L.J. 271 (2009); Alan O. Sykes, Corporate Liability for Extraterritorial Torts Under the Alien Tort Statute and Beyond: An Economic Analysis, 100 Georgetown L.J. 2161 (2012).

Kiobel generated significant commentary. For an effort to situate ATS litigation "within the traditional federal-courts framework of implied rights of action and federal common law," see Ernest A. Young, Universal Jurisdiction, the Alien Tort Statute, and Transnational Public Law Litigation After *Kiobel*, 64 Duke L.J. 1023 (2015). Young contends that this framework supports the Supreme Court's disallowance in *Kiobel* of "universal jurisdiction" under the ATS. For additional discussion of the decision and its implications, see the Symposium articles in Volume 89, Issue 4 of the Notre Dame Law

Review: Roger P. Alford, The Future of Human Rights Litigation After *Kiobel*, 89 Notre Dame L. Rev. 749 (2014); Anthony J. Bellia Jr. & Bradford R. Clark, Two Myths About the Alien Tort Statute, 89 Notre Dame L. Rev. 1609 (2014); William R. Casto, The ATS Cause of Action is *Sui Generis*, 89 Notre Dame L. Rev. 1545 (2014); Doug Cassell, Suing Americans for Human Rights Torts Overseas: The Supreme Court Leaves the Door Open, 89 Notre Dame L. Rev. 1773 (2014); William S. Dodge, Alien Tort Statute Litigation: The Road Not Taken, 89 Notre Dame L. Rev. 1577 (2014); Eugene Kontorovich, *Kiobel* Surprise: Unexpected by Scholars but Consistent with International Trends, 89 Notre Dame L. Rev. 1671 (2014); Thomas H. Lee, Three Lives of the Alien Tort Statute: The Evolving Role of the Judiciary in U.S. Foreign Relations, 89 Notre Dame L. Rev. 1645 (2014); Ralph G. Steinhardt, Determining Which Human Rights Claims "Touch and Concern" the United States: Justice Kennedy's *Filartiga*, 89 Notre Dame L. Rev. 1695 (2014); Beth Stephens, The Curious History of the Alien Tort Statute, 89 Notre Dame L. Rev. 1467 (2014); Carlos M. Vázquez, Things We Do with Presumptions: Reflections on *Kiobel v. Royal Dutch Petroleum*, 89 Notre Dame L. Rev. 1719 (2014). See also Roger P. Alford, Human Rights After *Kiobel*: Choice of Law and the Rise of Transnational Tort Litigation, 63 Emory L.J. 1089 (2014); Seth Davis & Christopher A. Whytock, State Remedies for Human Rights, 98 B.U. L. Rev. 397 (2018).

CHAPTER III

JUDICIAL REVIEW AND JUSTICIABILITY

SECTION 2. STANDING

SUBSECTION A. CONSTITUTIONAL CORE

Page 306, add a footnote at the end of the last paragraph:

^c For a critique of the "one-plaintiff rule" pursuant to which the Supreme Court and the lower federal courts have felt free in multiple-plaintiff cases to resolve the merits with respect to all of the plaintiffs as long as they find that at least one plaintiff has standing, see Aaron-Andrew P. Bruhl, One Good Plaintiff is Not Enough, 67 Duke L.J. 481 (2017).

Page 307, add at the end of Note 5:

James E. Pfander, Standing, Litigable Interests, and Article III's Case-or-Controversy Requirement, 65 UCLA L. Rev. 170 (2018), explains that, "in the late eighteenth and early nineteenth century, federal courts were routinely exercising judicial power over claims of right that did not seek to remedy any injury (factual or otherwise) and did not necessitate the joinder of adverse parties" and that "[f]ederal courts continue to hear such matters today." Pfander contends that "[t]he ongoing willingness of Congress to provide—and of the federal courts to accept—assignments of noncontentious jurisdiction makes it very hard to see how an across-the-board injury-in-fact or adverse-party requirement could be understood as a historically compelled element of the right of an individual to invoke the judicial power of the United States."

SUBSECTION B. STATUTORY STANDING

Page 325, add at the end of Note 6:

For an argument that the Thomas approach "is plausible and generally consistent with history and doctrine, and . . . provides an actual attempt at a way forward," see William Baude, Standing in the Shadow of Congress, 2016 Sup. Ct. Rev. 197.

Page 326, add to Note 8:

Randy Beck, Qui Tam Litigation Against Government Officials: Constitutional Implications of a Neglected History, 93 Notre Dame L. Rev. 1235, 1238 (2018) (relying on the Anglo-American tradition of using qui tam litigation to regulate public officials to "challenge[ ] *Lujan*'s conclusion that only the President or his subordinates may litigate generalized grievances about executive lawlessness").

SUBSECTION D. LEGISLATIVE AND GOVERNMENTAL STANDING

Page 360, add a new Note after Note 3:

3A. *VIRGINIA HOUSE OF DELEGATES V. BETHUNE-HILL*

In 2011, after the 2010 census, the State of Virginia redrew legislative districts for its Senate and House of Delegates. Voters in 12 of the impacted House districts sued two Virginia state agencies and four election officials, arguing that the redrawn districts were racially gerrymandered in violation of the Fourteenth Amendment's Equal Protection Clause. The Virginia House of Delegates (controlled by Republicans) and its Speaker (collectively "the House") intervened as defendants and defended the constitutionality of the challenged districts. A three-judge federal district court held that there had been unconstitutional racial gerrymandering in 11 of the districts and enjoined Virginia from conducting elections in the challenged districts until a new redistricting plan was adopted. A few weeks after the three-judge district court's ruling, Virginia's Attorney General (a Democrat) announced that the State would not pursue a direct appeal to the Supreme Court. The House, however, filed an appeal, which the defendants argued should be dismissed for lack of standing.

In Virginia House of Delegates v. Bethune-Hill, 587 U.S. ___, 139 S.Ct. ___ (2019), the Court held, in a five-four decision, that the House lacked standing to appeal. The lineup was unusual. The majority opinion was authored by Justice Ginsburg and was joined by Justices Thomas, Sotomayor, Kagan, and Gorsuch. Justice Alito dissented, joined by Chief Justice Roberts and Justices Breyer and Kavanaugh.

The majority first rejected the argument that the House had standing to represent the interests of the State of Virginia on appeal. Under Virginia law, the majority found, "[a]uthority and responsibility for representing the State's interests in civil litigation . . . rest exclusively with the State's Attorney General." The dissent did not address this issue. (Standing to represent the interests of a defendant on appeal is addressed further in Section E of this Chapter.)

Next, the majority held that the House lacked standing in its own right to defend the challenged districts. On this issue, the majority began by observing:

> To support standing, an injury must be "legally and judicially cognizable." Raines v. Byrd, 521 U.S. 811, 819 (1997). This Court has never held that a judicial decision invalidating a state law as unconstitutional inflicts a discrete, cognizable injury on each organ of government that participated in the law's passage. The Court's precedent thus lends no support for the notion that one House of a bicameral legislature, resting solely on its role in the legislative process, may appeal on its own behalf a judgment invalidating a state enactment.

The majority also noted that the Virginia constitution vests power over districting in the entire state legislature, not just the House. The fact that only the House was seeking to defend the legislature's prerogatives here, reasoned the majority, distinguished this case from *Arizona State Legislature:*

> In [*Arizona State Legislature*], . . . the Court recognized the standing of the Arizona House and Senate—*acting together*—to challenge a referendum that gave redistricting authority exclusively to an independent commission, thereby allegedly usurping the legislature's authority under the Federal Constitution over congressional redistricting. In contrast to this case, in *Arizona State Legislature* there was no mismatch between the body seeking to litigate and the body to which the relevant constitutional provision allegedly assigned exclusive redistricting authority. Just as individual members lack standing to assert the institutional interests of a legislature, see *Raines v. Byrd*, a single House of a bicameral legislature lacks capacity to assert interests belonging to the legislature as a whole.

The majority further distinguished *Arizona State Legislature* on the ground that the referendum in that case "was assailed on the ground that it permanently deprived the legislative plaintiffs of their role in the redistricting process. Here, by contrast, the challenged order does not alter the General Assembly's dominant initiating and ongoing role in redistricting." Nor did *Coleman v. Miller* support standing in this case, reasoned the majority, because "this case does not concern the results of a legislative chamber's poll or the validity of any counted or uncounted vote. At issue here, instead, is the constitutionality of a concededly enacted redistricting plan."

The majority then proceeded to reject the House's argument that it had standing because altered districts would affect its membership. In support of this argument, the House had relied on Sixty-seventh Minnesota State Senate v. Beens, 406 U.S. 187 (1972) (per curiam), in which the Court had allowed the Minnesota Senate to challenge a district court order concerning malapportionment that reduced the Senate's size from 67 to 35 members. The majority first observed that *Beens* predated decisions by the Court making clear that intervenor status is insufficient for standing to appeal, and it noted that "[w]hether *Beens* established law on the question of standing, as distinct from intervention, is thus less than pellucid." In any event, the majority said, *Beens* was distinguishable because "[c]utting the size of a legislative chamber in half would necessarily alter its day-to-day operations," whereas here the redistricting would only affect the identity of the members and "the House as an institution has no cognizable interest in the identity of its members."

Finally, the majority rejected the House's contention that it was harmed because a court order causing legislators to seek reelection in districts different from those that they currently represent would affect the House's representational nature. The majority noted that:

> [L]egislative districts change frequently—indeed, after every decennial census—and the Virginia Constitution resolves any confusion over which district is being represented. It provides that delegates continue to represent the districts that elected them, even if their reelection campaigns will be waged in different districts. Va. Const., Art. 2, § 6 ("A member in office at the time that a decennial redistricting law is enacted shall complete his term of office and shall continue to represent the district from which he was elected for the duration of such term of office . . . ."). We see little reason why the same would not hold true after districting changes caused by judicial decisions, and we thus foresee no representational confusion. And if harms centered on costlier or more difficult election campaigns are cognizable—a question that . . . we need not decide today—those harms would be suffered by individual legislators or candidates, not by the House as a body.

The majority concluded: "In short, Virginia would rather stop than fight on. One House of its bicameral legislature cannot alone continue the litigation against the will of its partners in the legislative process."

Justice Alito's dissent argued that redistricting would cause concrete harm to the House that should be sufficient to give it standing:

> A legislative districting plan powerfully affects a legislative body's output of work. Each legislator represents a particular district, and each district contains a particular set of constituents with particular interests and views. The interests and views of these constituents generally have an important effect on everything that a legislator does—meeting with the representatives of organizations and groups seeking the legislator's help in one way or another, drafting and sponsoring bills, pushing for and participating in hearings, writing or approving reports, and of course, voting. When the boundaries of a district are changed, the constituents and communities of interest present within the district are altered, and this is likely to change the way in which the district's representative does his or her work. And while every individual voter will end up being represented by a legislator no matter which districting plan is ultimately used, it matters a lot how voters with shared interests and views are concentrated or split up. The cumulative effects of all the decisions that go into a districting plan have an important impact on the overall work of the body. . . .

> It seems obvious that any group consisting of members who must work together to achieve the group's aims has a keen interest in the identity of its members, and it follows that the group also has a strong interest in how its members are selected. And what is more important to such a group than the content of its work? Apply what the Court says to a group other than a legislative body and it is immediately obvious that the Court is wrong. Does a string quartet have an interest in the identity of its cellist? Does a basketball team have an interest in the identity of its point guard? Does a board of directors have an interest in the identity of its chairperson? Does it

matter to these groups how their members are selected? Do these groups care if the selection method affects their performance? Of course.

On this point, the majority specifically responded to the dissent, arguing:

> [G]roups like the string quartet and basketball team posited by the dissent select their own members. . . . In stark contrast, the House does not select its own members. Instead, it is a representative body composed of members chosen by the people. Changes to its membership brought about by the voting public thus inflict no cognizable injury on the House.

Justice Alito concluded his dissent by suggesting that the majority was improperly influenced in its analysis by its views of the proper separation of powers structure at the federal level. He acknowledged that "[a]n interest asserted by a Member of Congress or by one or both Houses of Congress that is inconsistent with that structure may not be judicially cognizable," but he said that he did not "see how we can say anything similar about the standing of state legislators or state legislative bodies."

Page 361, add at the end of Note 4:

For a review of possible approaches to state standing, which concludes that "it is possible to recognize state standing in cases where a state suffers a significant injury without permitting every conceivable state suit against the federal government," see Bradford C. Mank, State Standing in *United States v. Texas*: Opening the Floodgates to States Challenging the Federal Government, or Proper Federalism?, 2018 U. Ill. L. Rev. 211.

Page 361, add new Notes after Note 4:

4A. *DEPARTMENT OF COMMERCE V. NEW YORK*

In Department of Commerce v. New York, 588 U.S. ___, 139 S.Ct. 2551 (2019), the Supreme Court considered a constitutional and statutory challenge to a decision by the Secretary of Commerce to reinstate a question about citizenship on the 2020 census. There were two groups of challengers. One group consisted of 18 States, the District of Columbia, various counties and cities, and the United States Conference of Mayors. The second group consisted of several non-governmental organizations that work with immigrant and minority communities. The challengers argued that reinstating a citizenship question would depress the census response rate by non-citizens and that this would in turn cause the challengers a variety of injuries, such as diminishment of political representation, loss of federal funds, degradation of census data, and diversion of resources.

Although the Court was divided on the merits, it unanimously agreed that at least some of the challengers—who were the respondents before the Supreme Court—had Article III standing. In an opinion by Chief Justice Roberts, the Court said:

> Several state respondents here have shown that if noncitizen households are undercounted by as little as 2%—lower than the District Court's 5.8% prediction—they will lose out on federal funds

that are distributed on the basis of state population. That is a sufficiently concrete and imminent injury to satisfy Article III, and there is no dispute that a ruling in favor of respondents would redress that harm.

In answer to the government's argument that any harm to the respondents would not be fairly traceable to the reinstatement of the census question because it would depend on the actions of third parties choosing not to respond to the census, the Court responded:

> [W]e are satisfied that, in these circumstances, respondents have met their burden of showing that third parties will likely react in predictable ways to the citizenship question, even if they do so unlawfully and despite the requirement that the Government keep individual answers confidential. The evidence at trial established that noncitizen households have historically responded to the census at lower rates than other groups, and the District Court did not clearly err in crediting the Census Bureau's theory that the discrepancy is likely attributable at least in part to noncitizens' reluctance to answer a citizenship question. Respondents' theory of standing thus does not rest on mere speculation about the decisions of third parties; it relies instead on the predictable effect of Government action on the decisions of third parties.

A majority of the Court then proceeded to uphold a decision by the District Court to remand the issue back to the Commerce Department because "the evidence tells a story that does not match the explanation the Secretary gave for his decision." The Trump administration then decided to omit the citizenship question from the census.

4B. Recent Litigation Under the "Emoluments Clauses"

There are two "Emoluments Clauses" in the Constitution. The Foreign Emoluments Clause, in Article I, Section 9, Clause 8, states that no federal official "shall, without the consent of the Congress, accept of any present, emolument, office, or title, of any kind whatever, from any king, prince, or foreign state." The Domestic Emoluments Clause, in Article II, Section 1, Clause 7, provides that "[t]he President shall, at stated Times, receive for his Services, a Compensation, which shall neither be encreased nor diminished during the Period for which he shall have been elected, and he shall not receive within that Period any other Emolument from the United States, or any of them."

President Trump has business holdings throughout the world, including hotels, restaurants, and resort properties. Although he turned over the management of these holdings to his sons shortly before taking office as President, he still benefits from them financially. If these holdings are receiving more patronage or other benefits from foreign governments as a result of him being President, it is arguable that he is receiving "emoluments" that have not been approved by Congress, in violation of the Foreign Emoluments Clause. In addition, his business has a long-term lease with the General Services Administration, an agency of the U.S. government, for a hotel property in Washington, D.C., and this arguably provides him with economic benefits that violate the Domestic Emoluments Clause. Furthermore, if the federal government or state governments patronize or provide benefits (such as tax concessions) to his properties, this may further violate the Domestic Emoluments Clause.

Several lawsuits have been brought against Trump, contending that he is violating the Emoluments Clauses and seeking declaratory and injunctive relief. These suits all implicate questions of standing. Appeals are pending in these cases, so the litigation will continue to develop. How do the cases fit with what the current law of standing? Which set of plaintiffs has the best case for standing? Is the district court's finding of standing in *Blumenthal v. Trump* consistent with *Raines v. Byrd*? If on appeal none of the plaintiffs in these cases is found to have standing, does this mean that the Emoluments Clauses are unenforceable?

(i)   Citizens for Responsibility and Ethics in Washington v. Trump

In Citizens for Responsibility and Ethics in Washington v. Trump, 276 F. Supp. 3d 174 (S.D.N.Y. 2017), the plaintiffs are a non-profit government watchdog organization, the Citizens for Responsibility and Ethics in Washington (CREW); an organization of restaurant employees; and two individuals involved in providing hotel and restaurant services. The District Court concluded that all of these plaintiffs lacked standing.

CREW argued that, because of Trump, it will now have to divert more of its resources and time to focusing on Emoluments Clause violations, and that this is an injury to the organization that gives it standing. The court rejected the argument, reasoning that:

> CREW alleges that the time, money, and attention it has diverted to this litigation from other projects have placed a significant drain on its limited resources. But such an allegation, by itself, is insufficient to establish an injury in fact. CREW's decision to investigate and challenge Defendant's actions . . . at the expense of its other initiatives reflects a choice about where and how to allocate its resources—one that almost all organizations with finite resources have to make. . . . If CREW could satisfy the standing requirement on this basis alone, it is difficult to see how any organization that claims it has directed resources to one project rather than another would not automatically have standing to sue.

The other plaintiffs, which the court referred to as the "Hospitality Plaintiffs," alleged that they were losing money because customers were being diverted to Trump's hotels and restaurants as a result of him being President. The District Court concluded that these plaintiffs lacked standing because they could not show that any economic injury they were suffering was fairly traceable to Trump's allegedly illegal conduct. The court stated:

> [I]t is wholly speculative whether the Hospitality Plaintiffs' loss of business is fairly traceable to Defendant's "incentives" or instead results from government officials' independent desire to patronize Defendant's businesses. Even before Defendant took office,

he had amassed wealth and fame and was competing against the Hospitality Plaintiffs in the restaurant and hotel business. It is only natural that interest in his properties has generally increased since he became President. As such, despite any alleged violation on Defendant's part, the Hospitality Plaintiffs may face a tougher competitive market overall. Aside from Defendant's public profile, there are a number of reasons why patrons may choose to visit Defendant's hotels and restaurants including service, quality, location, price and other factors related to individual preference. Therefore, the connection between the Hospitality Plaintiffs' alleged injury and Defendant's actions is too tenuous to satisfy Article III's causation requirement.

The court further reasoned that these plaintiffs should be denied standing on prudential grounds because they were not within the "zone of interests" of the Emoluments Clauses:

> Nothing in the text or the history of the Emoluments Clauses suggests that the Framers intended these provisions to protect anyone from competition. . . .
>
> [T]he intended purpose of the Foreign Emoluments Clause was to prevent official corruption and foreign influence, while the Domestic Emoluments Clause was meant to ensure presidential independence. Therefore, the Hospitality Plaintiffs' theory that the Clauses protect them from increased competition in the market for government business must be rejected, especially when (1) the Clauses offer no protection from increased competition in the market for *non-government* business and (2) with Congressional consent, the Constitution allows federal officials to accept foreign gifts and emoluments, *regardless* of its effect on competition. With Congress's consent, the Hospitality Plaintiffs could still face increased competition in the market for foreign government business but would have no cognizable claim to redress in court. There is simply no basis to conclude that the Hospitality Plaintiffs' alleged competitive injury falls within the zone of interests that the Emoluments Clauses sought to protect.

(ii) *District of Columbia v. Trump*

In District of Columbia v. Trump, 291 F. Supp. 3d 725 (D. Md. 2018), the plaintiffs are the District of Columbia and the state of Maryland. The court concluded that these plaintiffs had standing to challenge Trump's potential violations of the Emoluments Clauses in connection with his hotel in Washington, D.C. The court reasoned that D.C. and Maryland had adequately alleged three types of injuries relating to that hotel: to their "quasi-sovereign interests," because they felt pressured to grant concessions to or patronize the hotel or risk facing a competitive disadvantage vis-à-vis other states; to their "proprietary interests," because they have convention and conference centers that compete with the hotel; and to their "parens patriae interests" on behalf of their residents who participate in the hospitality industry and compete with the hotel. As for the requirement that the injury be traceable to the defendant's conduct, the court reasoned that:

> Plaintiffs have plausibly alleged they have been subjected to increased competition as a result of the President's purported violations. Their allegation is bolstered by explicit statements from certain foreign government officials indicating that they are clearly choosing to stay at the President's Hotel, because, as one representative of a foreign government has stated, they want him to know "I love your new hotel." . . .

The court also concluded that the plaintiffs fell within the "zone of interests" of the Emoluments Clauses, expressly disagreeing with the district court's analysis of that issue in the *CREW* case:

> [T]he Emoluments Clauses clearly were and are meant to protect all Americans. The President concedes as much. That being so, there is no reason why Plaintiffs, a subset of Americans who have demonstrated present injury or the immediate likelihood of injury by reason of the President's purported violations of the Emoluments Clauses, should be prevented from challenging what might be the President's serious disregard of the Constitution. Under the President's interpretation, it would seem that no one—save Congress which . . . may never undertake to act—would ever be able to enforce these constitutional provisions.

In explaining why it was allowing standing only with respect to the challenge to Trump's hotel in D.C., the court noted:

> There is good reason why [the plaintiffs'] standing should be recognized vis-à-vis the Hotel in Washington D.C., given the immediate impact on Plaintiffs in respect to the Hotel's operations. It is a considerable stretch, however, to find the requisite injury-in-fact to these particular Plaintiffs that is traceable to the Trump Organization's or, through it, the President's conduct outside the District of Columbia. How indeed, for instance, have Maryland or the District of Columbia suffered and how are they suffering immediate or impending injury as a result of whatever benefits the President might be deriving from foreign and state government patronage at the Trump Organization's Mar-a-Lago property in Florida or in the grant of patents to the Trump Organization or Trump relatives by China? In this respect, the Court, quite simply, sees neither immediate nor impending harm to Plaintiffs. Hence, the Court finds that these particular Plaintiffs lack standing to challenge the operations of the Trump Organization or the benefits the President may receive from its operations outside the District of Columbia. But to be perfectly clear: The Court reaches this conclusion only with respect to these Plaintiffs and the particular facts of the present case. This is in no way meant to say that other States or other businesses or individuals immediately affected by the same sort of violations alleged in the case at bar, e.g., a major hotel competitor in Palm Beach (near Mar-a-Lago) or indeed a hotel competitor anywhere in

the State of Florida, might not have standing to pursue litigation similar to that which is in process here.

On July 10, 2019, as this Supplement was going to press, the Fourth Circuit issued a writ of mandamus reversing the District Court's decision, concluding that the plaintiffs lacked standing. Terming the suit "extraordinary," the Fourth Circuit said that recognizing standing for any market participant who is allegedly injured by the unlawful advantage of a competitor would create a "boundless theory of standing." The claim of parens patriae standing to represent the economic interests of Maryland and D.C. simply restated the inadequate claim of competitor advantage, in the court's view. Finally, the court rejected the assertion of a "quasi-sovereign injury," saying that it amounted to "little more than a general interest in having the law followed." Review of the unanimous panel decision by the Fourth Circuit en banc or by the Supreme Court remains possible.

(iii) Blumenthal v. Trump

In Blumenthal v. Trump, 335 F. Supp. 3d 45 (D.D.C. 2018), the plaintiffs are approximately 200 members of Congress, from both the House and Senate. The court concluded that these legislators had standing to sue Trump for violations of the Foreign Emoluments Clause. It reasoned:

> In the context of legislator standing, the Supreme Court has recognized at least one type of institutional injury for which legislators may have standing to sue: complete vote nullification. . . .
>
> The [Foreign Emoluments] Clause requires the President to ask Congress before accepting a prohibited foreign emolument. Accepting the allegations in the Complaint as true, which the Court must at this juncture, the President is accepting prohibited foreign emoluments without asking and without receiving a favorable reply from Congress. . . . Plaintiffs adequately allege that the President has completely nullified their votes in the past because he has accepted prohibited foreign emoluments as though Congress had provided its consent. And he will completely nullify their votes in the future for the same reason, as plaintiffs allege that he intends to continue this practice.

The court rejected Trump's argument that the legislative process provided Congress with a sufficient remedy:

> [L]egislation on the emoluments issue does not provide an adequate remedy. First, in asking this Court to accept the proposition that legislation on the emoluments issue would be an adequate remedy, the President asks this Court to ignore this constitutional Clause. The Court may not do so. . . . The Clause is unambiguous: acceptance is prohibited without "Consent." U.S Const. art. I, § 9, cl. 8. The Clause therefore places the burden on the President to convince a majority of Members of Congress to consent. The legislation suggested by the President flips this burden, placing the burden on Members of Congress to convince a majority of their col-

leagues to enact the suggested legislation. This is not what the Clause requires.

Second, the President does not explain why such legislation, assuming he signed it, would prevent him from accepting prohibited foreign emoluments. His failure to explain is especially problematic given that the Constitution itself has not prevented him from allegedly accepting them. Third, the President does not explain how the proposed legislation would be adequate in view of the allegation that the President has not provided any information to Congress about the prohibited foreign emoluments he has received, and that he does not intend to change this practice. Legislating after Congress happens to learn about his acceptance of a prohibited foreign emolument through news reports is clearly an inadequate remedy. Fourth, legislation disagreeing with the President's acceptance of prohibited foreign emoluments does not provide a remedy for him already having allegedly accepted them without seeking and obtaining consent. Finally, legislation would neither prevent the President from accepting future prohibited foreign emoluments, nor force him to return those he has already accepted.

Furthermore, . . . Congress' appropriations power cannot be used to obtain a legislative remedy, such as refusing to appropriate funds for an Executive Branch program or for participation in a war, because there are no federal appropriations associated with the President's receipt of prohibited foreign emoluments.

SECTION 3. RELATED DOCTRINES

SUBSECTION B. RIPENESS

Page 420, omit footnote c:

[Explanation: The *Williamson* case was overruled in Knick v. Township of Scott, Pennsylvania, 588 U.S. ___, 139 S.Ct. 2162 (2019).]

SECTION 4. THE POLITICAL QUESTION

Page 470, add at the end of Note 1:

Consider the argument in John Harrison, The Political Question Doctrines, 67 Am. U. L. Rev. 457 (2017):

Nixon v. United States found substantial non-judicial finality under the political question rubric. Most likely the case means that Senate impeachments are absolutely conclusive as far as the courts are concerned, but the opinion can be read more narrowly. Each of the three leading cases in which the Court has relied on the political question doctrine—*Luther, Coleman,* and *Nixon v. United States*—rests on non-judicial finality. In all three, the Court found that the judiciary was absolutely bound by a political actor's decision that applied legal rules to specific facts.

Harrison notes that while there is Supreme Court "dicta that the political question doctrine limits the power of Article III courts to decide certain cases," there are several ways in which the doctrine has been employed in the cases, "none of which involves a lack of jurisdiction under Article III." One, for example, is a requirement that the Court accept an earlier political decision as a merits resolution of the dispute. Another is a bar on judicial relief that would interfere with a political decision. He concludes that the doctrine is a limit "on the judicial power but not on the cases Article III courts may decide." It "tells courts how to decide cases." Is there a practical difference between saying that a court is powerless to grant relief and saying that it is powerless to hear the case? In any event, has Harrison read *Nixon* correctly? Do the other political question cases in these materials fit this description?

A related question that could be asked is this: suppose a dispute that the federal courts cannot hear because of the political question doctrine was initiated in a state court. Would the state court be free to address the merits of federal questions raised in the suit independently of the political question doctrine? If it did so, would its judgment be reviewable by the Supreme Court?

Page 472, replace Note 3 on Political Gerrymandering, pages 472–74, with a new Main Case and Notes:

Rucho v. Common Cause

Supreme Court of the United States, 2019.
588 U.S. ___, 139 S.Ct. 2484.

■ CHIEF JUSTICE ROBERTS delivered the opinion of the Court.

Voters and other plaintiffs in North Carolina and Maryland challenged their States' congressional districting maps as unconstitutional partisan gerrymanders. The North Carolina plaintiffs complained that the State's districting plan discriminated against Democrats; the Maryland plaintiffs complained that their State's plan discriminated against Republicans. The plaintiffs alleged that the gerrymandering violated the First Amendment, the Equal Protection Clause of the Fourteenth Amendment, the Elections Clause, and Article I, § 2, of the Constitution. The District Courts in both cases ruled in favor of the plaintiffs, and the defendants appealed directly to this Court.

These cases require us to consider once again whether claims of excessive partisanship in districting are "justiciable"—that is, properly suited for resolution by the federal courts. This Court has not previously struck down a districting plan as an unconstitutional partisan gerrymander, and has struggled without success over the past several decades to discern judicially manageable standards for deciding such claims. The districting plans at issue here are highly partisan, by any measure. The question is whether the courts below appropriately exercised judicial power when they found them unconstitutional as well.

I

[In Part I, the Court summarized the facts and the litigation history of the decisions reported as Rucho v. Common Cause, 318 F. Supp. 3d 777 (M.D.N.C. 2018), and Lamone v. Benisek, 348 F. Supp. 3d 493 (Md. 2018). Both cases showed an energetic effort to draw congressional districts so as to gain partisan advantage, for Republicans in North Carolina and for Democrats in Maryland.]

II

A

. . . Chief Justice Marshall famously wrote that it is "the province and duty of the judicial department to say what the law is." Marbury v. Madison, 5 U.S. (1 Cranch) 137, 177 (1803). Sometimes, however, "the law is that the judicial department has no business entertaining the claim of unlawfulness—because the question is entrusted to one of the political branches or involves no judicially enforceable rights." Vieth v. Jubelirer, 541 U.S. 267, 277 (2004) (plurality opinion). In such a case the claim is said to present a "political question" and to be nonjusticiable—outside the courts' competence and therefore beyond the courts' jurisdiction. Baker v. Carr, 369 U.S. 186, 217 (1962). Among the political question cases the Court has identified are those that lack "judicially discoverable and manageable standards for resolving [them]." Id.

Last Term in Gill v. Whitford, 585 U.S. ___, 138 S.Ct. 1916 (2018), we reviewed our partisan gerrymandering cases and concluded that those cases "leave unresolved whether such claims may be brought." . . . The question here . . . is whether there is an "appropriate role for the Federal Judiciary" in remedying the problem of partisan gerrymandering—whether such claims are claims of legal right, resolvable according to legal principles, or political questions that must find their resolution elsewhere.

B

Partisan gerrymandering is nothing new. Nor is frustration with it. . . . In 1812, Governor of Massachusetts and future Vice President Elbridge Gerry notoriously approved congressional districts that the legislature had drawn to aid the Democratic-Republican Party. The moniker "gerrymander" was born when an outraged Federalist newspaper observed that one of the misshapen districts resembled a salamander. See Vieth, 541 U.S., at 274 (plurality opinion); Elmer C. Griffith, The Rise and Development of the Gerrymander 17–19 (1907). "By 1840, the gerrymander was a recognized force in party politics and was generally attempted in all legislation enacted for the formation of election districts. It was generally conceded that each party would attempt to gain power which was not proportionate to its numerical strength." Id. at 123.

The Framers addressed the election of Representatives to Congress in the Elections Clause. Art. I, § 4, cl. 1. That provision assigns to state legislatures the power to prescribe the "Times, Places and Manner of holding Elections" for Members of Congress, while giving Congress the power to "make or alter" any such regulations. . . .

Congress has regularly exercised its Elections Clause power, including to address partisan gerrymandering. The Apportionment Act of 1842, which required single member districts for the first time, specified that those districts be "composed of contiguous territory," Act of June 25, 1842, ch. 47, 5 Stat. 491, in "an attempt to forbid the practice of the gerrymander," Griffith, supra, at 12. Later statutes added requirements of compactness and equality of population. (Only the single member district requirement remains in place today. 2 U.S.C. § 2c.) . . .

Appellants suggest that, through the Elections Clause, the Framers set aside electoral issues such as the one before us as questions that only Congress can resolve. See *Baker*, 369 U.S. at 217. We do not agree. In two areas—one-person, one-vote and racial gerrymandering—our cases have held that there is a role for the courts with respect to at least some issues that could arise from a State's drawing of congressional districts. See Wesberry v. Sanders, 376 U.S. 1 (1964); Shaw v. Reno, 509 U.S. 630 (1993) (*Shaw I*).

But the history is not irrelevant. The Framers were aware of electoral districting problems and considered what to do about them. They settled on a characteristic approach, assigning the issue to the state legislatures, expressly checked and balanced by the Federal Congress. . . . At no point was there a suggestion that the federal courts had a role to play. Nor was there any indication that the Framers had ever heard of courts doing such a thing.

C

Courts have nevertheless been called upon to resolve a variety of questions surrounding districting. Early on, doubts were raised about the competence of the federal courts to resolve those questions. See Wood v. Broom, 287 U.S. 1 (1932); Colegrove v. Green, 328 U.S. 549 (1946).

In the leading case of *Baker v. Carr*, supra, voters in Tennessee complained that the State's districting plan for state representatives "debase[d]" their votes, because the plan was predicated on a 60-year-old census that no longer reflected the distribution of population in the State. The plaintiffs argued that votes of people in overpopulated districts held less value than those of people in less populated districts, and that this inequality violated the Equal Protection Clause of the Fourteenth Amendment. The District Court dismissed the action on the ground that the claim was not justiciable, relying on this Court's precedents, including *Colegrove*. This Court reversed. It identified various considerations relevant to determining whether a claim is a nonjusticiable political question, including whether there is "a lack of judicially discoverable and manageable standards for resolving it." 369 U.S. at 217. The Court concluded that the claim of population inequality among districts did not fall into that category, because such a claim could be decided under basic equal protection principles. Id. at 226. In *Wesberry v. Sanders*, the Court extended its ruling to malapportionment of congressional districts, holding that Article I, § 2, required that "one man's vote in a congressional election is to be worth as much as another's." 376 U.S. at 8.

Another line of challenges to districting plans has focused on race. Laws that explicitly discriminate on the basis of race, as well as those that are race neutral on their face but are unexplainable on grounds other than race, are of course presumptively invalid. The Court applied those principles to electoral boundaries in Gomillion v. Lightfoot, 364 U.S. 339 (1960), concluding that a challenge to an "uncouth twenty-eight sided" municipal boundary line that excluded black voters from city elections stated a constitutional claim. In Wright v. Rockefeller, 376 U.S. 52 (1964), the Court extended the reasoning of *Gomillion* to congressional districting.

Partisan gerrymandering claims have proved far more difficult to adjudicate. The basic reason is that, while it is illegal for a jurisdiction to depart from the one-person, one-vote rule, or to engage in racial discrimination in districting, "a jurisdiction may engage in constitutional political gerrymandering." Hunt v. Cromartie, 526 U.S. 541, 551 (1999). See also Gaffney v. Cummings, 412 U.S. 735, 753 (1973) (recognizing that "[p]olitics and political considerations are inseparable from districting and apportionment").

To hold that legislators cannot take partisan interests into account when drawing district lines would essentially countermand the Framers' decision to entrust districting to political entities. The "central problem" is not determining whether a jurisdiction has engaged in partisan gerrymandering. It is "determining when political gerrymandering has gone too far." *Vieth*, 541 U.S. at 296 (plurality opinion). See League of United Latin American Citizens v. Perry, 548 U.S. 399, 420 (2006) (*LULAC*) (opinion of Kennedy, J.) (difficulty is "providing a standard for deciding how much partisan dominance is too much"). . . .

[I]n Davis v. Bandemer, 478 U.S. 109, 116–17 (1986) (plurality opinion), we addressed a claim that Indiana Republicans had cracked and packed Democrats in violation of the Equal Protection Clause. A majority of the Court agreed that the case was justiciable, but the Court splintered over the proper standard to apply. Four Justices would have required proof of "intentional discrimination against an identifiable political group and an actual discriminatory effect on that group." Id. at 127. Two Justices would have focused on "whether the boundaries of the voting districts have been distorted deliberately and arbitrarily to achieve illegitimate ends." Id. at 165 (Powell, J., concurring in part and dissenting in part). Three Justices, meanwhile, would have held that the Equal Protection Clause simply "does not supply judicially manageable standards for resolving purely political gerrymandering claims." Id. at 147 (O'Connor, J., concurring in judgment). At the end of the day, there was 'no 'Court' for a standard that properly should be applied in determining whether a challenged redistricting plan is an unconstitutional partisan political gerrymander." Id. at 185 n.25 (opinion of Powell, J.). In any event, the Court held that the plaintiffs had failed to show that the plan violated the Constitution.

Eighteen years later, in *Vieth*, the plaintiffs complained that Pennsylvania's legislature "ignored all traditional redistricting criteria, including the preservation of local government boundaries," in order to benefit Republican congressional candidates. 541 U.S. at 272–73 (plurality opinion) (brackets omitted). Justice Scalia wrote for a four-Justice plurality. He would have held that the plaintiffs' claims were nonjusticiable because there was no "judicially discernible and manageable standard" for deciding them. Id. at 306. Justice Kennedy, concurring in the judgment, noted "the lack of comprehensive and neutral principles for drawing electoral boundaries [and] the absence of rules to limit and confine judicial intervention." Id. at 306–07. He nonetheless left open the possibility that "in another case a standard might emerge." Id. at 312. Four Justices dissented.

In *LULAC*, the plaintiffs challenged a mid-decade redistricting map approved by the Texas Legislature. Once again a majority of the Court could not find a justiciable standard for resolving the plaintiffs' partisan gerrymandering claims. See 548 U.S. at 414. . . .

III

A

In considering whether partisan gerrymandering claims are justiciable, we are mindful of Justice Kennedy's counsel in *Vieth*: Any standard for resolving such claims must be grounded in a "limited and precise rationale" and be "clear, manageable, and politically neutral." 541 U.S. at 306–08 (opinion concurring in judgment). An important reason for those careful constraints is that, as a Justice with extensive experience in state and local politics put it,"[t]he opportunity to control the drawing of electoral boundaries through the legislative process of apportionment is a critical and traditional part of politics in the United States." *Bandemer*, 478 U.S. at 145 (opinion of O'Connor, J.). An expansive standard requiring "the correction of all election district lines drawn for partisan reasons would commit federal and state courts to unprecedented intervention in the American political process," *Vieth*, 541 U.S. at 306 (opinion of Kennedy, J.).

As noted, the question is one of degree: How to "provid[e] a standard for deciding how much partisan dominance is too much." *LULAC*, 548 U.S. at 420 (opinion of Kennedy, J.). And it is vital in such circumstances that the Court act only in accord with especially clear standards: "With uncertain limits, intervening courts—even when proceeding with best intentions—would risk assuming political, not legal, responsibility for a process that often produces ill will and distrust." *Vieth*, 541 U.S. at 307 (opinion of Kennedy, J.). If federal courts are to "inject [themselves] into the most heated partisan issues" by adjudicating partisan gerrymandering claims, *Bandemer*, 478 U.S. at 145 (opinion of O'Connor, J.), they must be armed with a standard that can reliably differentiate unconstitutional from "constitutional political gerrymandering." Hunt v. Cromartie, 526 U.S. 541, 551 (1999).

B

Partisan gerrymandering claims rest on an instinct that groups with a certain level of political support should enjoy a commensurate level of political power and influence. Explicitly or implicitly, a districting map is alleged to be unconstitutional because it makes it too difficult for one party to translate statewide support into seats in the legislature. But such a claim is based on a "norm that does not exist" in our electoral system—"statewide elections for representatives along party lines." *Bandemer*, 478 U.S. at 159 (opinion of O'Connor, J.).

Partisan gerrymandering claims invariably sound in a desire for proportional representation. As Justice O'Connor put it, such claims are based on "a conviction that the greater the departure from proportionality, the more suspect an apportionment plan becomes." Id. "Our cases, however, clearly foreclose any claim that the Constitution requires proportional representation or that legislatures in reapportioning must draw district lines to come as near as possible to allocating seats to the contending parties in proportion to what their anticipated statewide vote will be." Id. at 130 (plurality opinion).

The Founders certainly did not think proportional representation was required. For more than 50 years after ratification of the Constitution, many States elected their congressional representatives through at-large or "general ticket" elections. Such States typically sent single-party delegations to Congress. That meant that a party could garner nearly half of the vote statewide and wind up without any seats in the congressional delegation....

Unable to claim that the Constitution requires proportional representation outright, plaintiffs inevitably ask the courts to make their own political judgment about how much representation particular political parties *deserve*—based on the votes of their supporters—and to rearrange the challenged districts to achieve that end. But federal courts are not equipped to apportion political power as a matter of fairness, nor is there any basis for concluding that they were authorized to do so. As Justice Scalia put it for the plurality in *Vieth*, 541 U.S. at 291:

> "Fairness" does not seem to us a judicially manageable standard.... Some criterion more solid and more demonstrably met than that seems to us necessary to enable the state legislatures to discern the limits of their districting discretion, to meaningfully constrain the discretion of the courts, and to win public acceptance for the courts' intrusion into a process that is the very foundation of democratic decisionmaking.

The initial difficulty in settling on a "clear, manageable and politically neutral" test for fairness is that it is not even clear what fairness looks like in this context. There is a large measure of "unfairness" in any winner-take-all system. Fairness may mean a greater number of competitive districts. Such a claim seeks to undo packing and cracking so that supporters of the disadvantaged party have a better shot at electing their preferred candidates. But making as many districts as possible more competitive could be a recipe for disaster for the disadvantaged party. As Justice White has pointed out, "[i]f all or most of the districts are competitive . . . even a narrow statewide preference for either party would produce an overwhelming majority for the winning party in the state legislature." *Bandemer*, 478 U.S. at 130 (plurality opinion).

On the other hand, perhaps the ultimate objective of a "fairer" share of seats in the congressional delegation is most readily achieved by yielding to the gravitational pull of proportionality and engaging in cracking and packing, to ensure each party its "appropriate" share of "safe" seats. Such an approach, however, comes at the expense of competitive districts and of individuals in districts allocated to the opposing party.

Or perhaps fairness should be measured by adherence to "traditional" districting criteria, such as maintaining political subdivisions, keeping communities of interest together, and protecting incumbents. See Brief for Bipartisan Group of Current and Former Members of the House of Representatives as Amici Curiae. But protecting incumbents, for example, enshrines a particular partisan distribution. And the "natural political geography" of a State—such as the fact that urban electoral districts are often dominated by one political party—can itself lead to inherently packed districts. As Justice Kennedy has explained, traditional criteria such as compactness and contiguity "cannot promise political neutrality . . . ." *Vieth*, 541 U.S. at 308–09 (opinion concurring in judgment).

Deciding among just these different visions of fairness (you can imagine many others) poses basic questions that are political, not legal. There are no legal standards discernible in the Constitution for making such judgments, let alone limited and precise standards that are clear, manageable, and politically neutral. Any judicial decision on what is "fair" in this context would be an "unmoored determination" of the sort characteristic of a political question beyond the competence of the federal courts.

And it is only after determining how to define fairness that you can even begin to answer the determinative question: "How much is too much?" At what point does permissible partisanship become unconstitutional? If compliance with traditional districting criteria is the fairness touchstone, for example, how much deviation from those criteria is constitutionally acceptable and how should mapdrawers prioritize competing criteria? Should a court "reverse gerrymander" other parts of a State to counteract "natural" gerrymandering caused, for example, by the urban concentration of one party? If a districting plan protected half of the incumbents but redistricted the rest into head to head races, would that be constitutional? A court would have to rank the relative importance of those traditional criteria and weigh how much deviation from each to allow.

If a court instead focused on the respective number of seats in the legislature, it would have to decide the ideal number of seats for each party and determine at what point deviation from that balance went too far. If a 5–3 allocation corresponds most closely to statewide vote totals, is a 6–2 allocation permissible, given that legislatures have the authority to engage in a certain degree of partisan gerrymandering? Which seats should be packed and which cracked? Or if the goal is as many competitive districts as possible, how close does the split need to be for the district to be considered competitive? Presumably not all districts could qualify, so how to choose? Even assuming the court knew which version of fairness to be looking for, there are no discernible and manageable standards for deciding whether there has been a violation. The questions are "unguided and ill suited to the development of judicial standards," *Vieth*, 541 U.S. at 296 (plurality opinion), and "results from one gerrymandering case to the next would likely be disparate and inconsistent," id. at 308 (opinion of Kennedy, J.).

Appellees contend that if we can adjudicate one-person, one-vote claims, we can also assess partisan gerrymandering claims. But the one-person, one-vote rule is relatively easy to administer as a matter of math. The same cannot be said of partisan gerrymandering claims, because the Constitution supplies no objective measure for assessing whether a districting map treats a political party fairly. . . .

More fundamentally, "vote dilution" in the one-person, one-vote cases refers to the idea that each vote must carry equal weight. In other words, each representative must be accountable to (approximately) the same number of constituents. That requirement does not extend to political parties. It does not mean that each party must be influential in proportion to its number of supporters. As we stated unanimously in *Gill*, "this Court is not responsible for vindicating generalized partisan preferences. The Court's constitutionally prescribed role is to vindicate the individual rights of the people appearing before it." 585 U.S. at ___, 138 S.Ct. at 1933.*

Nor do our racial gerrymandering cases provide an appropriate standard for assessing partisan gerrymandering. "[N]othing in our case law compels the conclusion that racial and political gerrymanders are subject to precisely the same constitutional scrutiny. In fact, our country's long and persistent history of racial discrimination in voting—as

---

* The dissent's observation that the Framers viewed political parties "with deep suspicion, as fomenters of factionalism and symptoms of disease in the body politic" is exactly right. Its inference from that fact is exactly wrong. The Framers would have been amazed at a constitutional theory that guarantees a certain degree of representation to political parties.

well as our Fourteenth Amendment jurisprudence, which always has reserved the strictest scrutiny for discrimination on the basis of race—would seem to compel the opposite conclusion." *Shaw I*, 509 U.S. at 650 (citation omitted). Unlike partisan gerrymandering claims, a racial gerrymandering claim does not ask for a fair share of political power and influence, with all the justiciability conundrums that entails. It asks instead for the elimination of a racial classification. A partisan gerrymandering claim cannot ask for the elimination of partisanship.

IV

Appellees and the dissent propose a number of "tests" for evaluating partisan gerrymandering claims, but none meets the need for a limited and precise standard that is judicially discernible and manageable. And none provides a solid grounding for judges to take the extraordinary step of reallocating power and influence between political parties.

A

The *Common Cause* District Court concluded that all but one of the districts in North Carolina's 2016 Plan [the districting plan challenged in the litigation] violated the Equal Protection Clause by intentionally diluting the voting strength of Democrats. In reaching that result the court first required the plaintiffs to prove "that a legislative mapdrawer's predominant purpose in drawing the lines of a particular district was to 'subordinate adherents of one political party and entrench a rival party in power.'" The District Court next required a showing "that the dilution of the votes of supporters of a disfavored party in a particular district—by virtue of cracking or packing—is likely to persist in subsequent elections such that an elected representative from the favored party in the district will not feel a need to be responsive to constituents who support the disfavored party." Finally, after a prima facie showing of partisan vote dilution, the District Court shifted the burden to the defendants to prove that the discriminatory effects are "attributable to a legitimate state interest or other neutral explanation."

The District Court's "predominant intent" prong is borrowed from the racial gerrymandering context. In racial gerrymandering cases, we rely on a "predominant intent" inquiry to determine whether race was, in fact, the reason particular district boundaries were drawn the way they were. If district lines were drawn for the purpose of separating racial groups, then they are subject to strict scrutiny because "race-based decisionmaking is inherently suspect." Miller v. Johnson, 515 U.S. 900, 915 (1995). But determining that lines were drawn on the basis of partisanship does not indicate that the districting was improper. A permissible intent—securing partisan advantage—does not become constitutionally impermissible, like racial discrimination, when that permissible intent "predominates."

The District Court tried to limit the reach of its test by requiring plaintiffs to show, in addition to predominant partisan intent, that vote dilution "is likely to persist" to such a degree that the elected representative will feel free to ignore the concerns of the supporters of the minority party. But "[t]o allow district courts to strike down apportionment plans on the basis of their prognostications as to the outcome of future elections . . . invites 'findings' on matters as to which neither judges nor anyone else can have any confidence." *Bandemer*, 478 U.S. at 160 (opinion of O'Connor, J.). . . .

Experience proves that accurately predicting electoral outcomes is not so simple, either because the plans are based on flawed assumptions about voter preferences and behavior or because demographics and priorities change over time. In our two leading partisan gerrymandering cases themselves, the predictions of durability proved to be dramatically wrong. In 1981, Republicans controlled both houses of the Indiana Legislature as well as the governorship. Democrats challenged the state legislature districting map enacted by the Republicans. This Court in *Bandemer* rejected that challenge, and just months later the Democrats increased their share of House seats in the 1986 elections. Two years later the House was split 50–50 between Democrats and Republicans, and the Democrats took control of the chamber in 1990. Democrats also challenged the Pennsylvania congressional districting plan at issue in *Vieth*. Two years after that challenge failed, they gained four seats in the delegation, going from a 12–7 minority to an 11–8 majority. At the next election, they flipped another Republican seat.

Even the most sophisticated districting maps cannot reliably account for some of the reasons voters prefer one candidate over another, or why their preferences may change. Voters elect individual candidates in individual districts, and their selections depend on the issues that matter to them, the quality of the candidates, the tone of the candidates' campaigns, the performance of an incumbent, national events or local issues that drive voter turnout, and other considerations. Many voters split their tickets. Others never register with a political party, and vote for candidates from both major parties at different points during their lifetimes. For all of those reasons, asking judges to predict how a particular districting map will perform in future elections risks basing constitutional holdings on unstable ground outside judicial expertise.

It is hard to see what the District Court's third prong—providing the defendant an opportunity to show that the discriminatory effects were due to a "legitimate redistricting objective"—adds to the inquiry. The first prong already requires the plaintiff to prove that partisan advantage predominates. Asking whether a legitimate purpose other than partisanship was the motivation for a particular districting map just restates the question.

B

The District Courts also found partisan gerrymandering claims justiciable under the First Amendment, coalescing around a basic three-part test: proof of intent to burden individuals based on their voting history or party affiliation; an actual burden on political speech or associational rights; and a causal link between the invidious intent and actual burden. Both District Courts concluded that the districting plans at issue violated the plaintiffs' First Amendment right to association. The District Court in North Carolina relied on testimony that, after the 2016 Plan was put in place, the plaintiffs faced "difficulty raising money, attracting candidates, and mobilizing voters to support the political causes and issues such Plaintiffs sought to advance." Similarly, the District Court in Maryland . . . concluded that Republicans in the Sixth District "were burdened in fundraising, attracting volunteers, campaigning, and generating interest in voting."

To begin, there are no restrictions on speech, association, or any other First Amendment activities in the districting plans at issue. The plaintiffs are free to engage in those activities no matter what the effect of a plan may be on their district.

The plaintiffs' argument is that partisanship in districting should be regarded as simple discrimination against supporters of the opposing party on the basis of political viewpoint. Under that theory, any level of partisanship in districting would constitute an infringement of their First Amendment rights. . . . It provides no standard for determining when partisan activity goes too far.

As for actual burden, the slight anecdotal evidence found sufficient by the District Courts in these cases shows that this too is not a serious standard for separating constitutional from unconstitutional partisan gerrymandering. The District Courts relied on testimony about difficulty drumming up volunteers and enthusiasm. How much of a decline in voter engagement is enough to constitute a First Amendment burden? How many door knocks must go unanswered? How many petitions unsigned? How many calls for volunteers unheeded? . . .

These cases involve blatant examples of partisanship driving districting decisions. But the First Amendment analysis below offers no "clear" and "manageable" way of distinguishing permissible from impermissible partisan motivation. The *Common Cause* court embraced that conclusion, observing that "a judicially manageable framework for evaluating partisan gerrymandering claims need not distinguish an 'acceptable' level of partisan gerrymandering from 'excessive' partisan gerrymandering" because "the Constitution does not authorize state redistricting bodies to engage in such partisan gerrymandering." The decisions below prove the prediction of the *Vieth* plurality that "a First Amendment claim, if it were sustained, would render unlawful *all* consideration of political affiliation in districting," 541 U.S. at 294, contrary to our established precedent.

C

The dissent proposes using a State's own districting criteria as a neutral baseline from which to measure how extreme a partisan gerrymander is. The dissent would have us line up all the possible maps drawn using those criteria according to the partisan distribution they would produce. Distance from the "median" map would indicate whether a particular districting plan harms supporters of one party to an unconstitutional extent.

As an initial matter, it does not make sense to use criteria that will vary from State to State and year to year as the baseline for determining whether a gerrymander violates the Federal Constitution. The degree of partisan advantage that the Constitution tolerates should not turn on criteria offered by the gerrymanderers themselves. . . .

Even if we were to accept the dissent's proposed baseline, it would return us to "the original unanswerable question (How much political motivation and effect is too much?)." *Vieth*, 541 U.S. at 296–97 (plurality opinion). Would twenty percent away from the median map be okay? Forty percent? Sixty percent? Why or why not? (We appreciate that the dissent finds all the unanswerable questions annoying, but it seems a useful way to make the point.) The dissent's answer says it all: "This much is too much." That is not even trying to articulate a standard or rule.

The dissent argues that there are other instances in law where matters of degree are left to the courts. True enough. But those instances typically involve constitutional or statutory provisions or common law confining and guiding the exercise of judicial discretion. . . . Here, on the other hand, the Constitution provides no basis whatever to guide the exercise of judicial discretion. Common experience gives content to terms such as "substantial risk" or "substantial harm," but the same cannot be said of substantial deviation from a median map. There is no way to tell whether the prohibited deviation from that map should kick in at 25 percent or 75 percent or some other point. The only provision in the Constitution that specifically addresses the matter assigns it to the political branches. See Art. I, § 4, cl. 1.

D

The North Carolina District Court further concluded that the 2016 Plan violated the Elections Clause and Article I, § 2. We are unconvinced by that novel approach.

Article I, § 2, provides that "[t]he House of Representatives shall be composed of Members chosen every second Year by the People of the several States." The Elections Clause provides that "[t]he Times, Places and Manner of holding Elections for Senators and Representatives, shall be prescribed in each State by the Legislature thereof; but the Congress may at any time by Law make or alter such Regulations, except as to the Places of chusing Senators." Art. I, § 4, cl. 1.

The District Court concluded that the 2016 Plan exceeded the North Carolina General Assembly's Elections Clause authority because, among other reasons, "the Elections Clause did not empower State legislatures to disfavor the interests of supporters of a particular candidate or party in drawing congressional districts." The court further held that partisan gerrymandering infringes the right of "the People" to select their representatives. Before the District Court's decision, no court had reached a similar conclusion. In fact, the plurality in *Vieth* concluded—without objection from any other Justice—that neither § 2 nor § 4 of Article I "provides a judicially enforceable limit on the political considerations that the States and Congress may take into account when districting." 541 U.S. at 305.

The District Court nevertheless asserted that partisan gerrymanders violate "the core principle of [our] republican government" preserved in Art. I, § 2, "namely, that the voters should choose their representatives, not the other way around." That seems like an objection more properly grounded in the Guarantee Clause of Article IV, § 4, which "guarantee[s] to every State in [the] Union a Republican Form of Government." This Court has several times concluded, however, that the Guarantee Clause does not provide the basis for a justiciable claim. See, e.g., Pacific States Telephone & Telegraph Co. v. Oregon, 223 U.S. 118 (1912).

V

Excessive partisanship in districting leads to results that reasonably seem unjust. But the fact that such gerrymandering is "incompatible with democratic principles," Arizona State Legislature v. Arizona Independent Redistricting Commission, 576 U.S. at ___, 135 S.Ct. at 2658, does not mean that the solution lies with the federal judiciary. We conclude that partisan gerrymandering claims present political questions beyond the reach of the federal courts. Federal judges have no license to reallocate political power between the two major political parties, with no plausible grant of authority in the Constitution, and no legal standards to limit and direct their decisions. "[J]udicial action must be governed by *standard*, by *rule*," and must be "principled, rational, and based upon reasoned distinctions" found in the Constitution or laws. *Vieth*, 541 U.S. at 278, 279 (plurality opinion). Judicial review of partisan gerrymandering does not meet those basic requirements.

Today the dissent essentially embraces the argument that the Court unanimously rejected in *Gill*: "this Court can address the problem of partisan gerrymandering because it *must*." 585 U.S. at ___, 138 S.Ct. at 1929. That is not the test of our authority under the Constitution; that document instead "confines the federal courts to a properly judicial role." Town of Chester v. Laroe Estates, Inc., 581 U.S. ___, ___, 137 S.Ct. 1645, 1650 (2017).

What the appellees and dissent seek is an unprecedented expansion of judicial power. We have never struck down a partisan gerrymander as unconstitutional—despite various requests over the past 45 years. The expansion of judicial authority would not be into just any area of controversy, but into one of the most intensely partisan aspects of American political life. That intervention would be unlimited in scope and duration—it would recur over and over again around the country with each new round of districting, for state as well as federal representatives. Consideration of the impact of today's ruling on democratic principles cannot ignore the effect of the unelected and politically unaccountable branch of the Federal Government assuming such an extraordinary and unprecedented role.

Our conclusion does not condone excessive partisan gerrymandering. Nor does our conclusion condemn complaints about districting to echo into a void. The States, for example, are actively addressing the issue on a number of fronts. In 2015, the Supreme Court of Florida struck down that State's congressional districting plan as a violation of the Fair Districts Amendment to the Florida Constitution. League of Women Voters of Florida v. Detzner, 172 So. 3d 363 (2015). The dissent wonders why we can't do the same. The answer is that there is no "Fair Districts Amendment" to the Federal Constitution. Provisions in state statutes and state constitutions can provide standards and guidance for state courts to apply. . . . [N]umerous other States are restricting partisan considerations in districting through legislation. One way they are doing so is by placing power to draw electoral districts in the hands of independent commissions. . . .

Other States have mandated at least some of the traditional districting criteria for their mapmakers. Some have outright prohibited partisan favoritism in redistricting. . . .

As noted, the Framers gave Congress the power to do something about partisan gerrymandering in the Elections Clause. The first bill introduced in the 116th Congress would require States to create 15-member independent commissions to draw congressional districts and would establish certain redistricting criteria, including protection for communities of interest, and ban partisan gerrymandering. H.R. 1, 116th Cong., 1st Sess., §§ 2401, 2411 (2019).

Dozens of other bills have been introduced to limit reliance on political considerations in redistricting. . . .

[An] example is the Fairness and Independence in Redistricting Act, which was introduced in 2005 and has been reintroduced in every Congress since. That bill would require every State to establish an independent commission to adopt redistricting plans. The bill also set forth criteria for the independent commissions to use, such as compactness, contiguity, and population equality. It would prohibit consideration of voting history, political party affiliation, or incumbent Representative's residence. H.R. 2642, 109th Cong., 1st Sess., § 4 (referred to subcommittee).

We express no view on any of these pending proposals. We simply note that the avenue for reform established by the Framers, and used by Congress in the past, remains open.

* * *

No one can accuse this Court of having a crabbed view of the reach of its competence. But we have no commission to allocate political power and influence in the absence of a constitutional directive or legal standards to guide us in the exercise of such authority. "It is emphatically the province and duty of the judicial department to say what the law is." *Marbury v. Madison*, 10 U.S. at 177. In this rare circumstance, that means our duty is to say "this is not law."

The [judgments below] are vacated, and the cases are remanded with instructions to dismiss for lack of jurisdiction.

■ JUSTICE KAGAN, with whom JUSTICE GINSBURG, JUSTICE BREYER, and JUSTICE SOTOMAYOR join, dissenting.

For the first time ever, this Court refuses to remedy a constitutional violation because it thinks the task beyond judicial capabilities.

And not just any constitutional violation. The partisan gerrymanders in these cases deprived citizens of the most fundamental of their constitutional rights: the rights to participate equally in the political process, to join with others to advance political beliefs, and to choose their political representatives. In so doing, the partisan gerrymanders here debased and dishonored our democracy, turning upside-down the core American idea that all governmental power derives from the people. These gerrymanders enabled politicians to entrench themselves in office as against voters' preferences. They promoted partisanship above respect for the popular will. They encouraged a politics of polarization and dysfunction. If left unchecked, gerrymanders like the ones here may irreparably damage our system of government.

And checking them is *not* beyond the courts. The majority's abdication comes just when courts across the country, including those below, have coalesced around manageable judicial standards to resolve partisan gerrymandering claims. Those standards satisfy the majority's own benchmarks. They do not require—indeed, they do not permit—courts to rely on their own ideas of electoral fairness, whether proportional representation or any other. And they limit courts to correcting only egregious gerrymanders, so judges do not become omnipresent players in the political process. But yes, the standards used here do allow—as well they should—judicial intervention in the worst-of-the-worst cases of democratic subversion, causing blatant constitutional harms. In other words, they allow courts to undo partisan gerrymanders of the kind we face today from North Carolina and Maryland. In giving such gerrymanders a pass from judicial review, the majority goes tragically wrong.

I

Maybe the majority errs in these cases because it pays so little attention to the constitutional harms at their core. After dutifully reciting each case's facts, the majority leaves them forever behind, instead immersing itself in everything that could conceivably go amiss if courts became involved. [At this point and in Part I-A, Justice Kagan reviewed the facts in more detail than the Court had provided. Her point was to show that naked partisan political advantage motivated the redistricting decisions. She began her recitation of the details: "As I relate what happened in those two States, ask yourself: Is this how American democracy is supposed to work?"]

B

Now back to the question I asked before: Is that how American democracy is supposed to work? I have yet to meet the person who thinks so.

"Governments," the Declaration of Independence states, "deriv[e] their just Powers from the Consent of the Governed." The Constitution begins: "We the People of the United States." The Gettysburg Address (almost) ends: "[G]overnment of the people, by the people, for the people." If there is a single idea that made our Nation (and that our Nation commended to the world), it is this one: The people are sovereign. The "power," James Madison wrote, "is in the people over the Government, and not in the Government over the people." 4 Annals of Cong. 934 (1794).

Free and fair and periodic elections are the key to that vision. The people get to choose their representatives. And then they get to decide, at regular intervals, whether to keep them. . . . Election day—next year, and two years later, and two years after that—is what links the people to their representatives, and gives the people their sovereign power. That day is the foundation of democratic governance.

And partisan gerrymandering can make it meaningless. At its most extreme—as in North Carolina and Maryland—the practice amounts to "rigging elections." Vieth v. Jubelirer, 541 U.S. 267, 317 (2004) (Kennedy, J., concurring in judgment) (internal quotation marks omitted). By drawing districts to maximize the power of some voters and minimize the power of others, a party in office at the right time can entrench itself there for a decade or more, no matter what the voters would prefer. [P]oliticians can cherry-pick voters to ensure their reelection. . . .

The majority disputes none of this. I think it important to underscore that fact: The majority disputes none of what I have said (or will say) about how gerrymanders undermine democracy. Indeed, the majority concedes (really, how could it not?) that gerrymandering is "incompatible with democratic principles" (quoting Arizona State Legislature v. Arizona Independent Redistricting Commission, 576 U.S. ___, ___ 135 S.Ct. 2652, 2658 (2015)). And therefore what? That recognition would seem to demand a response. The majority offers two ideas that might qualify as such. One is that the political process can deal with the problem—a proposition so dubious on its face that I feel secure in delaying my answer for some time. The other is that political gerrymanders have always been with us. To its credit, the majority does not frame that point as an originalist constitutional argument. After all (as the majority rightly notes), racial and residential gerrymanders were also once with us, but the Court has done something about that fact. The majority's idea instead seems to be that if we have lived with partisan gerrymanders so long, we will survive.

That complacency has no cause. Yes, partisan gerrymandering goes back to the Republic's earliest days. (As does vociferous opposition to it.) But big data and modern technology—of just the kind that the mapmakers in North Carolina and Maryland used—make today's gerrymandering altogether different from the crude linedrawing of the past. Old-time efforts, based on little more than guesses, sometimes led to so-called dummymanders—gerrymanders that went spectacularly wrong. Not likely in today's world. Mapmakers now have access to more granular data about party preference and voting behavior than ever before. County-level voting data has given way to precinct-level or city-block-level data; and increasingly, mapmakers avail themselves of data sets providing wideranging information about even individual voters. Just as important, advancements in computing technology have enabled mapmakers to put that information to use with unprecedented efficiency and precision. While bygone mapmakers may have drafted three or four alternative districting plans, today's mapmakers can generate thousands of possibilities at the touch of a key—and then choose the one giving their party maximum advantage (usually while still meeting traditional districting requirements). The effect is to make gerrymanders far more effective and durable than before, insulating politicians against all but the most titanic shifts in the political tides. These are not your grandfather's—let alone the Framers'—gerrymanders. . . .

C

Partisan gerrymandering of the kind before us not only subverts democracy (as if that weren't bad enough). It violates individuals' constitutional rights as well. That statement is not the lonesome cry of a dissenting Justice. This Court has recognized extreme partisan gerrymandering as such a violation for many years.

Partisan gerrymandering operates through vote dilution—the devaluation of one citizen's vote as compared to others. A mapmaker draws district lines to "pack" and "crack" voters likely to support the disfavored party. He packs supermajorities of those voters into a relatively few districts, in numbers far greater than needed for their preferred candidates to prevail. Then he cracks the rest across many more districts, spreading them so thin that their candidates will not be able to win. Whether the person is packed or cracked, his vote carries less weight—has less consequence—than it would under a neutrally drawn (non-partisan) map. In short, the mapmaker has made some votes count for less, because they are likely to go for the other party.

That practice implicates the Fourteenth Amendment's Equal Protection Clause. The Fourteenth Amendment, we long ago recognized, "guarantees the opportunity for equal participation by all voters in the election" of legislators. Reynolds v. Sims, 377 U.S. 533, 566 (1964). And that opportunity "can be denied by a debasement or dilution of the weight of a citizen's vote just as effectively as by wholly prohibiting the free exercise of the franchise." Id. at 555. Based on that principle, this Court in its one-person-one-vote decisions prohibited creating districts with significantly different populations. A State could not, we explained, thus "dilut[e] the weight of votes because of place of residence." Id. at 566. The constitutional injury in a partisan gerrymandering case is much the same, except that the dilution is based on party affiliation. In such a case, too, the districters have set out to reduce the weight of certain citizens' votes, and thereby deprive them of their capacity to "full[y] and effective[ly] participat[e] in the political process[ ]." Id. at 565. As Justice Kennedy (in a controlling opinion) once hypothesized: If districters declared that they were drawing a map "so as most to burden [the votes of] Party X's" supporters, it would violate the Equal Protection Clause. *Vieth*, 541 U.S. at 312. For (in the language of the one-person-one-vote decisions) it would infringe those voters' rights to "equal [electoral] participation." *Reynolds*, 377 U.S. at 566.

And partisan gerrymandering implicates the First Amendment too. That Amendment gives its greatest protection to political beliefs, speech, and association. Yet partisan gerrymanders subject certain voters to "disfavored treatment"—again, counting their votes for less—precisely because of "their voting history [and] their expression of political views." *Vieth*, 541 U.S. at 314 (opinion of Kennedy, J.). And added to that strictly personal harm is an associational one. Representative democracy is "unimaginable without the ability of citizens to band together in [support of] candidates who espouse their political views." California Democratic Party v. Jones, 530 U.S. 567, 574 (2000). By diluting the votes of certain citizens, the State frustrates their efforts to translate those affiliations into political effectiveness. In both those ways, partisan gerrymanders of the kind we confront here undermine the protections of "democracy embodied in the First Amendment." Elrod v. Burns, 427 U.S. 347, 357 (1976) (internal quotation marks omitted).

Though different Justices have described the constitutional harm in diverse ways, nearly all have agreed on this much: Extreme partisan gerrymandering (as happened in North Carolina and Maryland) violates the Constitution. Once again, the majority never disagrees; it appears to accept the "principle that each person must have an equal say in the election of representatives." And indeed, without this settled and shared understanding that cases like these inflict constitutional injury, the question of whether there are judicially manageable standards for resolving them would never come up.

II

So the only way to understand the majority's opinion is as follows: In the face of grievous harm to democratic governance and flagrant infringements on individuals' rights—in the face of escalating partisan manipulation whose compatibility with this Nation's values and law no one defends—the majority declines to provide any remedy. For the first time in this Nation's history, the majority declares that it can do nothing about an acknowledged constitutional violation because it has searched high and low and cannot find a workable legal standard to apply.

The majority gives two reasons for thinking that the adjudication of partisan gerrymandering claims is beyond judicial capabilities. First and foremost, the majority says, it cannot find a neutral baseline—one not based on contestable notions of political fairness—from which to measure injury. According to the majority, "[p]artisan gerrymandering claims invariably sound in a desire for proportional representation." But the Constitution does not mandate proportional representation. So, the majority contends, resolving those claims "inevitably" would require courts to decide what is "fair" in the context of districting. They would have "to make their own political judgment about how much representation particular political parties *deserve*" and "to rearrange the challenged districts to achieve that end." And second, the majority argues that even after establishing a baseline, a court would have no way to answer "the determinative question: 'How much is too much?'" No "discernible and manageable" standard is available, the majority claims—and so courts could willy-nilly become embroiled in fixing every districting plan.

I'll give the majority this one—and important—thing: It identifies some dangers everyone should want to avoid. Judges should not be apportioning political power based on their own vision of electoral fairness, whether proportional representation or any other. And judges should not be striking down maps left, right, and center, on the view that every smidgen of politics is a smidgen too much. Respect for state legislative processes—and restraint in the exercise of judicial authority—counsels intervention in only egregious cases.

But in throwing up its hands, the majority misses something under its nose: What it says can't be done *has* been done. Over the past several years, federal courts across the country—including, but not exclusively, in the decisions below—have largely converged on a standard for adjudicating partisan gerrymandering claims (striking down both Democratic and Republican districting plans in the process). And that standard does what the majority says is impossible. The standard does not use any judge-made conception of electoral fairness—either proportional representation or any other; instead, it takes as its baseline a State's own criteria of fairness, apart from partisan gain. And by requiring plaintiffs to make difficult showings relating to both purpose and effects, the standard invalidates the most extreme, but only the most extreme, partisan gerrymanders. . . .

A

Start with the standard the lower courts used. . . . Both courts focused on the harm of vote dilution, though the North Carolina court mostly grounded its analysis in the Fourteenth Amendment and the

Maryland court in the First. And both courts (like others around the country) used basically the same three-part test to decide whether the plaintiffs had made out a vote dilution claim. As many legal standards do, that test has three parts: (1) intent; (2) effects; and (3) causation. First, the plaintiffs challenging a districting plan must prove that state officials' "predominant purpose" in drawing a district's lines was to "entrench [their party] in power" by diluting the votes of citizens favoring its rival. Second, the plaintiffs must establish that the lines drawn in fact have the intended effect by "substantially" diluting their votes. And third, if the plaintiffs make those showings, the State must come up with a legitimate, non-partisan justification to save its map. If you are a lawyer, you know that this test looks utterly ordinary. It is the sort of thing courts work with every day.

Turn now to the test's application. First, did the North Carolina and Maryland districters have the predominant purpose of entrenching their own party in power? Here, the two District Courts catalogued the overwhelming direct evidence that they did. . . .

The majority's response to the District Courts' purpose analysis is discomfiting. The majority does not contest the lower courts' findings; how could it? Instead, the majority says that state officials' intent to entrench their party in power is perfectly "permissible," even when it is the predominant factor in drawing district lines. But that is wrong. True enough, that the intent to inject "political considerations" into districting may not raise any constitutional concerns. In Gaffney v. Cummings, 412 U.S. 735 (1973), for example, we thought it nonproblematic when state officials used political data to ensure rough proportional representation between the two parties. And true enough that even the naked purpose to gain partisan advantage may not rise to the level of constitutional notice when it is not the driving force in mapmaking or when the intended gain is slight. See *Vieth*, 541 U.S. at 286 (plurality opinion). But when political actors have a specific and predominant intent to entrench themselves in power by manipulating district lines, that goes too far. . . .

On to the second step of the analysis, where the plaintiffs must prove that the districting plan substantially dilutes their votes. The majority fails to discuss most of the evidence the District Courts relied on to find that the plaintiffs had done so. But that evidence—particularly from North Carolina—is the key to understanding both the problem these cases present and the solution to it they offer. The evidence reveals just how bad the two gerrymanders were (in case you had any doubts). And it shows how the same technologies and data that today facilitate extreme partisan gerrymanders also enable courts to discover them, by exposing just how much they dilute votes.

Consider the sort of evidence used in North Carolina first. There, the plaintiffs demonstrated the districting plan's effects mostly by relying on what might be called the "extreme outlier approach." (Here's a spoiler: the State's plan was one.) The approach—which also has recently been used in Michigan and Ohio litigation—begins by using advanced computing technology to randomly generate a large collection of districting plans that incorporate the State's physical and political geography and meet its declared districting criteria, except for partisan gain. For each of those maps, the method then uses actual precinct-level votes from past elections to determine a partisan outcome (i.e., the number of Democratic and Republican seats that map produces). Suppose we now have 1,000 maps, each with a partisan outcome attached to it. We can line up those maps on a continuum—the most favorable to Republicans on one end, the most favorable to Democrats on the other. We can then find the median outcome—that is, the outcome smack dab in the center—in a world with no partisan manipulation. And we can see where the State's actual plan falls on the spectrum—at or near the median or way out on one of the tails? The further out on the tail, the more extreme the partisan distortion and the more significant the vote dilution.

Using that approach, the North Carolina plaintiffs offered a boatload of alternative districting plans—all showing that the State's map was an out-out-out-outlier. One expert produced 3,000 maps, adhering in the way described above to the districting criteria that the North Carolina redistricting committee had used, other than partisan advantage. To calculate the partisan outcome of those maps, the expert also used the same election data (a composite of seven elections) that [had been] employed when devising the North Carolina plan in the first instance. The results were, shall we say, striking. Every single one of the 3,000 maps would have produced at least one more Democratic House Member than the State's actual map, and 77% would have elected three or four more. A second expert obtained essentially the same results with maps conforming to more generic districting criteria (e.g., compactness and contiguity of districts). Over 99% of that expert's 24,518 simulations would have led to the election of at least one more Democrat, and over 70% would have led to two or three more. Based on those and other findings, the District Court determined that the North Carolina plan substantially dilutes the plaintiffs' votes.

Because the Maryland gerrymander involved just one district, the evidence in that case was far simpler—but no less powerful for that. . . .

The majority claims all these findings are mere "prognostications" about the future, in which no one "can have any confidence." But the courts below did not gaze into crystal balls, as the majority tries to suggest. Their findings about these gerrymanders' effects on voters—both in the past and predictably in the future—were evidence-based, data-based, statistics-based. Knowledge-based, one might say. The courts did what anyone would want a decisionmaker to do when so much hangs in the balance. They looked hard at the facts, and they went where the facts led them. They availed themselves of all the information that mapmakers . . . and politicians . . . work so hard to amass and then use to make every districting decision. They refused to content themselves with unsupported and out-of-date musings about the unpredictability of the American voter. They did not bet America's future—as today the majority does—on the idea that maps constructed with so much expertise and care to make electoral outcomes impervious to voting would somehow or other come apart. They looked at the evidence—at the facts about how these districts operated—and they could reach only one conclusion. By substantially diluting the votes of citizens favoring their rivals, the politicians of one party had succeeded in entrenching themselves in office. They had beat democracy.

B

The majority's broadest claim, as I've noted, is that this is a price we must pay because judicial oversight of partisan gerrymandering cannot be "politically neutral" or "manageable." Courts, the majority argues, will have to choose among contested notions of electoral fairness. (Should they take as the ideal mode of districting proportional representation, many competitive seats, adherence to traditional districting criteria, or so forth?) And even once courts have chosen, the majority continues, they will have to decide "[h]ow much is too much?"—that is, how much deviation from the chosen "touchstone" to allow? In answering that question, the majority surmises, they will likely go far too far. So the whole thing is impossible, the majority concludes. To prove its point, the majority throws a bevy of question marks on the page. (I count nine in just two paragraphs.) But it never tries to analyze the serious question presented here—whether the kind of standard developed below falls prey to those objections, or instead allows for neutral and manageable oversight. The answer, as you've already heard enough to know, is the latter. That kind of oversight is not only possible; it's been done.

Consider neutrality first. Contrary to the majority's suggestion, the District Courts did not have to—and in fact did not—choose among competing visions of electoral fairness. That is because they did not try to compare the State's actual map to an "ideally fair" one (whether based on proportional representation or some other criterion). Instead, they looked at the difference between what the State did and what the State would have done if politicians hadn't been intent on partisan gain. Or put differently, the comparator (or baseline or touchstone) is the result not of a judge's philosophizing but of the State's own characteristics and judgments. . . . All the courts did was determine how far the State had gone off that track because of its politicians' effort to entrench themselves in office.

The North Carolina litigation well illustrates the point. The thousands of randomly generated maps I've mentioned formed the core of the plaintiffs' case that the North Carolina plan was an "extreme[ ] outlier." Those maps took the State's political landscape as a given. In North Carolina, for example, Democratic voters are highly concentrated in cities. That fact was built into all the maps; it became part of the baseline. On top of that, the maps took the State's legal landscape as a given. They incorporated the State's districting priorities, excluding partisanship. So in North Carolina, for example, all the maps adhered to the traditional criteria of contiguity and compactness. But the comparator maps in another State would have incorporated different objectives—say, the emphasis Arizona places on competitive districts or the requirement Iowa imposes that counties remain whole. The point is that the assemblage of maps, reflecting the characteristics and judgments of the State itself, creates a neutral baseline from which to assess whether partisanship has run amok. Extreme outlier as to what? As to the other maps the State could have produced given its unique political geography and its chosen districting criteria. *Not* as to the maps a judge, with his own view of electoral fairness, could have dreamed up. . . .

The majority's sole response misses the point. According to the majority, "it does not make sense to use" a State's own (non-partisan) districting criteria as the baseline from which to measure partisan gerrymandering because those criteria "will vary from State to State and year to year." But that is a virtue, not a vice—a feature, not a bug. Using the criteria the State itself has chosen at the relevant time prevents any judicial predilections from affecting the analysis—exactly what the majority claims it wants. At the same time, using those criteria enables a court to measure just what it should: the extent to which the pursuit of partisan advantage—by these legislators at this moment—has distorted the State's districting decisions. Sure, different non-partisan criteria could result, as the majority notes, in different partisan distributions to serve as the baseline. But that in itself raises no issue: Everyone agrees that state officials using non-partisan criteria (e.g., must counties be kept together? should districts be compact?) have wide latitude in districting. The problem arises only when legislators or mapmakers substantially deviate from the baseline distribution by manipulating district lines for partisan gain. So once again, the majority's analysis falters because it equates the demand to eliminate partisan gerrymandering with a demand for a single partisan distribution—the one reflecting proportional representation. But those two demands are different, and only the former is at issue here.

The majority's "how much is too much" critique fares no better than its neutrality argument. How about the following for a first-cut answer: This much is too much. By any measure, a map that produces a greater partisan skew than any of 3,000 randomly generated maps (all with the State's political geography and districting criteria built in) reflects "too much" partisanship. Think about what I just said: The absolute worst of 3,001 possible maps. . . . Even the majority acknowledges that "[t]hese cases involve blatant examples of partisanship driving districting decisions." If the majority had done nothing else, it could have set the line here. How much is too much? At the least, any gerrymanders as bad as these.

And if the majority thought that approach too case-specific, it could have used the lower courts' general standard—focusing on "predominant" purpose and "substantial" effects—without fear of indeterminacy. I do not take even the majority to claim that courts are incapable of investigating whether legislators mainly intended to seek partisan advantage. That is for good reason. Although purpose inquiries carry certain hazards (which courts must attend to), they are a common form of analysis in constitutional cases. See, e.g., Miller v. Johnson, 515 U.S. 900, 916 (1995); Church of Lukumi Babalu Aye, Inc. v. Hialeah, 508 U.S. 520, 533 (1993); Washington v. Davis, 426 U.S. 229, 239 (1976). Those inquiries would be no harder here than in other contexts.

Nor is there any reason to doubt, as the majority does, the competence of courts to determine whether a district map "substantially" dilutes the votes of a rival party's supporters from the everything-but-partisanship baseline described above. . . . As this Court recently noted, "the law is full of instances" where a judge's decision rests on "estimating rightly . . . some matter of degree"—including the "substantial[ity]" of risk or harm. Johnson v. United States, 576 U.S. ___, ___, 135 S.Ct. 2551, 2561 (2015) (internal quotation marks omitted). . . . [C]ourts all the time make judgments about the substantiality of harm without reducing them to particular percentages. If courts are no longer competent to do so, they will have to relinquish, well, substantial portions of their docket.

And the combined inquiry used in these cases set the bar high, so that courts could intervene in the worst partisan gerrymanders, but no others. Or to say the same thing, so that courts could intervene in the kind of extreme gerrymanders that nearly every Justice for decades has thought to violate the Constitution. Illicit purpose was simple to show here only because politicians and mapmakers thought their actions could not be attacked in court. They therefore felt free to openly proclaim their intent to entrench their party in office. But if the Court today had declared that behavior justiciable, such smoking guns would all but disappear. Even assuming some officials continued to try implementing extreme partisan gerrymanders, they would not brag about their efforts. So plaintiffs would have to prove the intent to entrench through circumstantial evidence—essentially showing that no other explanation (no geographic feature or non-partisan districting objective) could explain the districting plan's vote dilutive effects. And that would be impossible unless those effects were even more than substantial—unless mapmakers had packed and cracked with abandon in unprecedented ways. As again, they did here. That the two courts below found constitutional violations does not mean their tests were unrigorous; it means that the conduct they confronted was constitutionally appalling—by even the strictest measure, inordinately partisan.

The majority, in the end, fails to understand both the plaintiffs' claims and the decisions below. Everything in today's opinion assumes that these cases grew out of a "desire for proportional representation" or, more generally phrased, a "fair share of political power." And everything in it assumes that the courts below had to (and did) decide what that fair share would be. But that is not so. The plaintiffs objected to one specific practice—the extreme manipulation of district lines for partisan gain. Elimination of that practice could have led to proportional representation. Or it could have led to nothing close. What was left after the practice's removal could have been fair, or could have been unfair, by any number of measures. That was not the crux of this suit. The plaintiffs asked only that the courts bar politicians from entrenching themselves in power by diluting the votes of their rivals' supporters. And the courts, using neutral and manageable—and eminently legal—standards, provided that (and only that) relief. This Court should have cheered, not overturned, that restoration of the people's power to vote.

III

This Court has long understood that it has a special responsibility to remedy violations of constitutional rights resulting from politicians' districting decisions. . . . [T]he need for judicial review is at its most urgent in cases like these. "For here, politicians' incentives conflict with voters' interests, leaving citizens without any political remedy for their constitutional harms." *Gill*, 585 U.S. at ___, 138 S.Ct. at 1941 (Kagan, J., concurring). Those harms arise because politicians want to stay in office. No one can look to them for effective relief.

The majority disagrees, concluding its opinion with a paean to congressional bills limiting partisan gerrymanders. "Dozens of [those] bills have been introduced," the majority says. One was "introduced in 2005 and has been reintroduced in every Congress since." And might be reintroduced until the end of time. Because what all these bills have in common is that they are not laws. The politicians who benefit from partisan gerrymandering are unlikely to change partisan gerrymandering. And because those politicians maintain themselves in office through partisan gerrymandering, the chances for legislative reform are slight.

No worries, the majority says; it has another idea. The majority notes that voters themselves have recently approved ballot initiatives to put power over districting in the hands of independent commissions or other nonpartisan actors. . . . Fewer than half the States offer voters an opportunity to put initiatives to direct vote; in all the rest (including North Carolina and Maryland), voters are dependent on legislators to make electoral changes (which for all the reasons already given, they are unlikely to do). . . .

The majority's most perplexing "solution" is to look to state courts. . . . But what do those courts know that this Court does not? If they can develop and apply neutral and manageable standards to identify unconstitutional gerrymanders, why couldn't we?

We could have, and we should have. The gerrymanders here—and they are typical of many—violated the constitutional rights of many hundreds of thousands of American citizens. Those voters (Republicans in the one case, Democrats in the other) did not have an equal opportunity to participate in the political process. Their votes counted for far less than they should have because of their partisan affiliation. When faced with such constitutional wrongs, courts must intervene: "It is emphatically the province and duty of the judicial department to say what the law is." Marbury v. Madison, 10 U.S. (1 Cranch) 137, 177 (1803). That is what the courts below did. Their decisions are worth a read. They (and others that have recently remedied similar violations) are detailed, thorough, painstaking. They evaluated with immense care the factual evidence and legal arguments the parties presented. They used neutral and manageable and strict standards. They had not a shred of politics about them. Contra the majority, this *was* law.

That is not to deny, of course, that these cases have great political consequence. They do. Among the amicus briefs here is one from a bipartisan group of current and former Members of the House of Representatives. They describe all the ways partisan gerrymandering harms our political system—what they call "a cascade of negative results." These artificially drawn districts shift influence from swing voters to party-base voters who participate in primaries; make bipartisanship and pragmatic compromise politically difficult or impossible; and drive voters away from an ever more dysfunctional political process. Last year, we heard much the same from current and former state legislators. In their view, partisan gerrymandering has "sounded the death-knell of bipartisanship," creating a legislative environment that is "toxic" and "tribal." Brief as Amicus Curiae in *Gill v. Whitford*, O.T. 2016, No.16–1161, pp. 6, 25. Gerrymandering, in short, helps create the polarized political system so many Americans loathe. . . .

Of all times to abandon the Court's duty to declare the law, this was not the one. The practices challenged in these cases imperil our system of government. Part of the Court's role in that system is to defend its foundations. None is more important than free and fair elections. With respect but deep sadness, I dissent.

QUESTIONS AND COMMENTS ON *RUCHO V. COMMON CAUSE*

In *Rucho*, the majority concludes that "partisan gerrymandering claims present political questions beyond the reach of the federal courts." But did the majority in effect decide that partisan gerrymandering is constitutional? It reasons, for example, that the Constitution does not require proportional representation and that there are "no legal standards discernible in the Constitution" for making judgments about fairness in this context. What is added (or subtracted) by calling this a political question? Is the majority's contention that its holding "does not condone excessive partisan gerrymandering" persuasive?

Kagan's dissent argues that there are judicially manageable standards for addressing the worst cases of partisan gerrymandering. Is she persuasive? She emphasizes in particular the approach that had been used in the North Carolina litigation, which she calls the "extreme outlier approach." What reasons does the majority give for rejecting that approach? Is Justice Kagan's response effective?

What impact, if any, does *Rucho* have on the ability of state courts to hear challenges to partisan gerrymandering? Given that state courts are not bound by the limitations of Article III, could they adjudicate federal constitutional challenges to partisan gerrymandering that cannot be adjudicated in the federal courts? Or is the Court's analysis based on more than just the limits of Article III? In any event, can state courts hear challenges to partisan gerrymandering based on *state* constitutional law?

Finally, consider the lineup. The Court was presented with challenges to partisan gerrymandering by both Democrats (in Maryland) and Republicans (in North Carolina). Why was the Court divided along traditional ideological lines?

CHAPTER IV

CONGRESSIONAL CONTROL OF THE FEDERAL COURTS

SECTION 1. POWER TO LIMIT FEDERAL COURT JURISDICTION

Page 515, add to the first paragraph of Note 9:

Daniel D. Birk, The Common-Law Exceptions Clause: Congressional Control of Supreme Court Appellate Jurisdiction in Light of British Precedent, 63 Vill. L. Rev. 189 (2018);

Page 515, add at the end of the first paragraph in Note 9:

For consideration of Congress's power to strip *state* courts of jurisdiction to hear federal claims, and the conclusion that, although Congress has broad power to do so in many instances, it lacks the authority to "simultaneously close both state and federal courts to federal constitutional challenges to state laws," see Michael C. Dorf, Congressional Power to Strip State Courts of Jurisdiction, 97 Tex. L. Rev. 1 (2018).

SECTION 2. POWER TO REGULATE FEDERAL RULES OF DECISION AND JUDGMENTS

Page 547, add a new Note after Note 10:

10A. *PATCHAK V. ZINKE*

The Court again considered a congressional intervention into pending litigation in Patchak v. Zinke, 583 U.S. ___, 138 S.Ct. 897 (2018). In that case, the federal government had taken into trust a parcel of land in Michigan known as the "Bradley Property" for the benefit of an Indian tribe, so that the tribe could operate a casino there. In doing so, the government relied on statutory authority conferred in the 1934 Indian Reorganization Act. A neighboring landowner, David Patchak, sued the Secretary of the Interior, arguing that the government lacked authority under the Act to take the property into trust because the Indian tribe in question had not been formally recognized by the government until long after the Act was passed. The case made its way up to the Supreme Court, and the Court held that Patchak had standing to bring the suit and that the suit fell within a statutory exception to the government's sovereign immunity. The Court remanded for further proceedings.

While the case was pending on remand in the District Court, Congress passed the Gun Lake Act, 128 Stat. 1913. Section 2(a) of the Act provides that the Bradley Property "is reaffirmed as trust land, and the actions of the Secretary of the Interior in taking that land into trust are ratified and confirmed." Section 2(b) provides: "Notwithstanding any other provision of law, an action (including an action pending in a Federal court as of the date of enactment of this Act) relating to the land described in subsection (a) shall not be filed or maintained in a Federal court and shall be promptly dismissed." Based on this Act, the District Court dismissed the case, and the Court of Appeals affirmed.

In a splintered decision, the Supreme Court affirmed, rejecting Patchak's argument that Section 2(b) of the Act violated Article III of the Constitution. Justice Thomas, writing for himself and Justices Breyer, Alito, and Kagan, reasoned that Congress has broad authority both to strip federal court jurisdiction and to change the statutory law applicable to a pending case:

> Section 2(b) changes the law. Specifically, it strips federal courts of jurisdiction over actions "relating to" the Bradley Property. Before the Gun Lake Act, federal courts had jurisdiction to hear these actions. See 28 U.S.C. § 1331. Now they do not. This kind of legal change is well within Congress's authority and does not violate Article III. . . .
>
> Statutes that strip jurisdiction "chang[e] the law" for the purpose of Article III, [Plaut v. Spenthrift Farm, Inc., 514 U.S. 211, 218 (1995)], just as much as other exercises of Congress's legislative authority. Article I permits Congress "[t]o constitute Tribunals inferior to the supreme Court," § 8, and Article III vests the judicial power "in one supreme Court, and in such inferior Courts as the Congress may from time to time ordain and establish," § 1. These provisions reflect the so-called Madisonian Compromise, which resolved the Framers' disagreement about creating lower federal courts by leaving that decision to Congress. . . . Congress's greater power to create lower federal courts includes its lesser power to "limit the jurisdiction of those Courts." United States v. Hudson, 11 U.S. (7 Cranch) 32, 33 (1812). So long as Congress does not violate other constitutional provisions, its "control over the jurisdiction of the federal courts" is "plenary." Trainmen v. Toledo, P. & W. R. Co., 321 U.S. 50, 63–64 (1944).

Relying on *Ex parte McCardle*, Thomas also noted that "this Court has held that Congress generally does not violate Article III when it strips federal jurisdiction over a class of cases." While acknowledging that the Court in *McCardle* observed that another avenue of Supreme Court review remained available, Thomas contended that the Court was making that observation to address a potential problem under the Habeas Suspension Clause, not a potential problem under Article III. Thomas further argued that the present case was distinguishable from *United States v. Klein* because in *Klein* "Congress had no authority to declare that pardons are not evidence of loyalty, so it could not achieve the same result by stripping jurisdiction whenever claimants cited pardons as evidence of loyalty. Nor could Congress confer jurisdiction to a federal court but then strip jurisdiction from that same court once the court concluded that a pardoned claimant should prevail under the statute." Section 2(b) of the Gun Lake Act, by contrast, "does not attempt to exercise a power that the Constitution vests in another branch. And unlike the selective jurisdiction-stripping statute in *Klein*, § 2(b) strips jurisdiction over every suit relating to the Bradley Property." Quoting from *Bank Markazi*, Thomas observed that "a statute does not impinge on judicial power when it directs courts to apply a new legal standard to undisputed facts."

Finally, Thomas rejected the argument that Section 2(b) of the Act interfered with the federal judicial power in violation of *Plaut v. Spendthrift Farm, Inc.* Unlike in *Plaut*, the litigation in this case had not been concluded when Congress acted. "As this Court emphasized in *Plaut*," Justice Thomas noted, "Article III does not prohibit Congress from enacting new laws that apply to pending civil cases. . . . This principle applies equally to statutes that strip jurisdiction." In answer to the dissent's concern that Congress had targeted a specific case and directed its outcome, Thomas doubted that this presented a constitutional problem, and, in any event, he disagreed with this characterization of what Congress had done: "Nothing on the face of § 2(b) is limited to Patchak's case, or even to his challenge under the Indian Reorganization Act. Instead, the text extends to all suits 'relating to' the Bradley Property."

Justice Breyer added a separate concurrence to emphasize that Section 2(a) of the Act, the validity of which was not challenged, makes clear that the Secretary of the Interior had authority to keep the Bradley Property in trust, and that Section 2(b) merely supplements that provision: "The second part, the jurisdictional part, perhaps gilds the lily, perhaps simplifies judicial decisionmaking (the judge need only determine whether a lawsuit relates to the Bradley Property), but, read in context, it does no more than provide an alternative legal standard for courts to apply that seeks the same real-world result as does the first part: The Bradley Property shall remain in trust."

Joined by Justice Sotomayor, Justice Ginsburg concurred in the judgment but did not join Thomas's plurality opinion. Ginsburg reasoned that in this case Congress had simply retracted its waiver of sovereign immunity: "Just as it is Congress's prerogative to consent to suit, so too is it within Congress's authority to withdraw consent once given."

Justice Sotomayor also wrote separately to note that she agreed with a number of points in the dissent: "I agree with the dissent that Congress may not achieve through jurisdiction stripping what it cannot permissibly achieve outright, namely, directing entry of judgment for a particular party. I also agree that an Act that merely deprives federal courts of jurisdiction over a single proceeding is not enough to be considered a change in the law and that any statute that portends to do so should be viewed with great skepticism." She did not join the dissent, she explained, because she agreed with Justice Ginsburg that the Gun Lake Act "should not be read to strip the federal courts of jurisdiction but rather to restore the Federal Government's sovereign immunity."

Chief Justice Roberts dissented and was joined by Justices Kennedy and Gorsuch. Roberts contended that "Congress has previously approached the boundary between legislative and judicial power, but it has never gone so far as to target a single party for adverse treatment and direct the precise disposition of his pending case. Section 2(b)—remarkably—does just that." Unlike the plurality, Roberts said that he "would hold that Congress exercises the judicial power when it manipulates jurisdictional rules to decide the outcome of a particular pending case. Because the Legislature has no authority to direct entry of judgment for a party, it cannot achieve the same result by stripping jurisdiction over a particular proceeding." Roberts also argued that *McCardle* should not be "[r]ead for all it is worth" and that such an expansive reading would be inconsistent with *Klein*. Roberts concluded: "[A]lthough the stakes of this particular dispute may seem insignificant, the principle that the plurality would enshrine is of historic consequence. In no uncertain terms, the plurality disavows any limitations on Congress's power to determine judicial results, conferring on the Legislature a colonial-era authority to pick winners and losers in pending litigation as it pleases."

What does this decision suggest about the scope of Congress's authority to strip federal court jurisdiction over a pending case? Note that four of the Justices endorse some constitutional limits on jurisdiction-stripping: the three dissenters, and Justice Sotomayor. By contrast, the four Justices in the plurality appear to view Congress's authority to strip jurisdiction as essentially plenary. Justice Ginsburg's position on the issue is not clear. How easy would it be for courts to administer the proposed constitutional limitation articulated by the dissent? Is Justice Breyer right that, in any event, the case was effectively over as a result of Section 2(a) of the statute, given Congress's authority to change the statutory law applicable to a pending civil case?

SECTION 4. POWER TO CREATE NON-ARTICLE III COURTS

Page 575, add a footnote at the end of Note 2:

a For an argument that *Palmore* is wrong and that "[t]he original meaning of the Constitution, longstanding historical practice and precedent, and functional concerns all show that Article III's judicial protections should apply to courts in the capital," see James Durling, The District of Columbia and Article III, 107 Georgetown L.J. 1205 (2019).

Page 614, add new Notes after Note 3:

3A. REAFFIRMING THE PUBLIC RIGHTS DOCTRINE: *OIL STATES ENERGY SERVICES, LLC V. GREENE'S ENERGY GROUP, LLC*

The Patent and Trademark Office (PTO), an administrative agency, is responsible for issuing patents, based on a determination of whether the claims in the patent meet various statutory criteria. Since 1980, Congress has given the PTO the authority to conduct ex parte reexamination of patents it has issued. In 1999, Congress added a procedure called "inter partes reexamination," pursuant to which any person could file with the PTO a request for reexamination of a patent, and these requests would be resolved by the agency.

In 2012, Congress replaced inter partes reexamination with an adversarial process known as "inter partes review." Under this process, anyone other than the patent holder can petition for a review of the validity of patent claims. The decision whether to initiate the review is in the discretion of the Director of the PTO, but before doing so the Director must determine "that there is a reasonable likelihood that the petitioner would prevail with respect to at least 1 of the claims challenged."[a] Inter partes review proceedings are heard by the Patent Trial and Appeal Board, an adjudicatory body within the PTO that sits in three-member panels of administrative law patent judges. In the proceedings, the petitioner and the patent owner are entitled to certain discovery; to file affidavits, declarations, and written memoranda; and to receive an oral hearing before the Board. Appeals from Board decisions can be heard in the U.S. Court of Appeals for the Federal Circuit, an Article III court.

In 2001, Oil States Energy Services, LLC, an oilfield services company, obtained a patent relating to an apparatus and method for protecting wellhead equipment used in hydraulic fracturing. In 2012, it brought suit in a federal district court against a competing oilfield services company, Greene's Energy Group, LLC, for allegedly infringing the patent. While the case was pending, Greene's petitioned the PTO to institute inter partes review of the validity of two of Oil States' patent claims. The review was allowed to proceed, and the Board held that Oil States' two patent claims were invalid. Oil States appealed that decision to the Federal Circuit, challenging not only the merits of the Board's decision but also arguing that the inter partes review process violated both Article III of the Constitution and the Seventh Amendment. The Federal Circuit rejected these arguments.

In Oil States Energy Services, LLC v. Greene's Energy Group, LLC, 584 U.S. ___, 138 S.Ct. 1365 (2018), the Supreme Court affirmed. In an opinion by Justice Thomas, the Court explained that its precedents "have given Congress significant latitude to assign adjudication of public rights to entities other than Article III courts." While acknowledging that its decisions have not always been clear or consistent about the distinction between public and private rights, the Court stated that "[i]nter partes review falls squarely within the public-rights doctrine."

It is undisputed, said the Court, that the decision whether to *grant* a patent is a matter involving public rights. Such a decision, the Court explained, "has the key features to fall within this Court's longstanding formulation of the public-rights doctrine." In particular, the Court noted that patents involve a grant of rights from the government, these rights did not exist at common law and instead arise from statutes, and Congress and the executive branch have the constitutional authority to make such a grant without a judicial determination. The Court reasoned that "[i]nter partes review is simply a reconsideration of that grant, and Congress has permissibly reserved the PTO's authority to conduct that reconsideration." This review, the Court further noted, "involves the same basic matter as the grant of a patent. So it, too, falls on the public-rights side of the line." As a result, said the

---

[a] In SAS Institute Inc. v. Iancu, 584 U.S. ___, 138 S.Ct. 1348 (2018), the Supreme Court construed the relevant statute to require that, if the Director authorizes inter partes review, the review must extend to all claims raised by the petitioner.

Court, "[t]he Constitution does not prohibit the Board from resolving it outside of an Article III court."

As for the court-like powers exercised by the Board, the Court explained:

> [T]his Court has never adopted a "looks like" test to determine if an adjudication has improperly occurred outside of an Article III court. The fact that an agency uses court-like procedures does not necessarily mean it is exercising the judicial power. This Court has rejected the notion that a tribunal exercises Article III judicial power simply because it is "called a court and its decisions called judgments." Williams v. United States, 289 U.S. 553, 563 (1933). Nor does the fact that an administrative adjudication is final and binding on an individual who acquiesces in the result necessarily make it an exercise of the judicial power. See, e.g., Murray's Lessee v. Hoboken Land & Improvement Co., 59 U.S. 272, 280–81 (1856) (permitting the Treasury Department to conduct "final and binding" audits outside of an Article III court). Although inter partes review includes some of the features of adversarial litigation, it does not make any binding determination regarding "the liability of [Greene's Energy] to [Oil States] under the law as defined." Crowell v. Benson, 285 U.S. 22, 51 (1932). It remains a matter involving public rights, one "between the government and others, which from [its] nature do[es] not require judicial determination." Ex parte Bakelite Corp., 279 U.S. 438, 451 (1929).[5]

Its conclusion that the inter partes review process was consistent with Article III was also sufficient, the Court explained, to dispose of the Seventh Amendment challenge: "This Court's precedents establish that, when Congress properly assigns a matter to adjudication in a non-Article III tribunal, 'the Seventh Amendment poses no independent bar to the adjudication of that action by a nonjury factfinder.' Granfinanciera, S. A. v. Nordberg, 492 U.S. 33, 53–54 (1989)."

The Court concluded by emphasizing the "narrowness" of its holding:

> We address the constitutionality of inter partes review only. We do not address whether other patent matters, such as infringement actions, can be heard in a non-Article III forum. And because the Patent Act provides for judicial review by the Federal Circuit, we need not consider whether inter partes review would be constitutional "without any sort of intervention by a court at any stage of the proceedings," Atlas Roofing Co. v. Occupational Safety and Health Review Comm'n, 430 U.S. 442, 455 n.13 (1977). Moreover, we address only the precise constitutional challenges that Oil States raised here. Oil States does not challenge the retroactive application of inter partes review, even though that procedure was

---

[5] Oil States also points out that inter partes review "is initiated by private parties and implicates no waiver of sovereign immunity." Brief for Petitioner 30–31. But neither of those features takes inter partes review outside of the public-rights doctrine. . . . Also, inter partes review is not initiated by private parties in the way that a common-law cause of action is. To be sure, a private party files the petition for review. But the decision to institute review is made by the Director and committed to his unreviewable discretion.

not in place when its patent issued. Nor has Oil States raised a due process challenge. Finally, our decision should not be misconstrued as suggesting that patents are not property for purposes of the Due Process Clause or the Takings Clause.

Justice Breyer, in a brief concurrence joined by Justices Ginsburg and Sotomayor, insisted that "the Court's opinion should not be read to say that matters involving private rights may never be adjudicated other than by Article III courts, say, sometimes by agencies. Our precedent is to the contrary."

Justice Gorsuch dissented and was joined by Chief Justice Roberts. Based on a review of various historical materials, Gorsuch contended that "only courts could hear patent challenges in England at the time of the founding," and he argued that this history should inform the interpretation of Article III. He also noted that, "from the time it established the American patent system in 1790 until about 1980, Congress left the job of invalidating patents at the federal level to courts alone." He rejected the argument that, because the grant of a patent is a public right, a decision to revoke a patent can be reserved to non-Article III adjudicators: "Just because you give a gift doesn't mean you forever enjoy the right to reclaim it." Gorsuch concluded:

> Today's decision may not represent a rout but it at least signals a retreat from Article III's guarantees. Ceding to the political branches ground they wish to take in the name of efficient government may seem like an act of judicial restraint. But enforcing Article III isn't about protecting judicial authority for its own sake. It's about ensuring the people today and tomorrow enjoy no fewer rights against governmental intrusion than those who came before. And the loss of the right to an independent judge is never a small thing. It's for that reason Hamilton warned the judiciary to take "all possible care . . . to defend itself against" intrusions by the other branches. The Federalist No. 78, at 466. It's for that reason I respectfully dissent.

3B. ORTIZ V. UNITED STATES

In Ortiz v. United States, 585 U.S. ___, 138 S.Ct. 2165 (2018), the Supreme Court held that it was constitutional for Congress to provide for Supreme Court review of decisions by the Court of Appeals for the Armed Forces (CAAF), a non-Article III military court. Although the parties had not questioned the Court's jurisdiction, a law professor, Aditya Bamzai, filed an amicus brief arguing that the Court lacked Article III authority to hear appeals from the CAAF. The Court gave significant attention to this argument but rejected it in a 7–2 decision. Justice Kagan, writing for the Court, reasoned that the "essential character" of the military court system is judicial; that it is well established that the Supreme Court can review the decisions of state courts, territorial courts, and D.C. courts, even though they are, like the CAAF, not Article III tribunals; and that, even though the CAAF resides within the executive branch, it is a judicial entity created by Congress. Kagan observed, however, that "[i]f Congress were to grant us appellate jurisdiction over decisions of newer entities advancing an administrative (rather than judicial) mission, the question would be different—and the answer not found in this opinion." Justice Thomas concurred, explaining that he agreed fully with the Court's decision but was writing separately "to explain why that conclusion is consistent with the Founders' understanding of judicial power—specifically, the distinction they drew between public and private rights." Justice Alito dissented and was joined by Justice Gorsuch. Alito reasoned that the Supreme Court's Article III appellate jurisdiction extends only to "review[ing] one thing: the lawful exercise of *judicial* power," and that "Executive Branch officers . . . cannot lawfully exercise the judicial power of any sovereign, no matter how court-like their decisionmaking process might appear." Because the CAAF is "an agent of executive power to aid the Commander in Chief," said Alito, "[i]t follows that our appellate jurisdiction does not permit us to review its decisions directly."

Page 618, add a new Note after Note 5:

5A. *LUCIA V. SECURITIES AND EXCHANGE COMMISSION*

Art. II, Sec. 2 of the Constitution defines the appointment powers of the President. Some senior appointments (judges, cabinet officers, etc.) are made by the President with the advice and consent of the Senate. For "all other Officers of the United States," Congress "may by Law vest the Appointment of such inferior Officers, as they think proper, in the President alone, in the Courts of Law, or in the Heads of Departments."

The question in Lucia v. Securities and Exchange Commission, 585 U.S. __, 138 S.Ct. 2044 (2018), was whether administrative law judges in the SEC are "Officers of the United States" within this description or whether they are mere "employees" of the federal government whose appointment is not controlled by any constitutional provision. The question arose in an administrative enforcement proceeding against the purveyor of a retirement savings plan called "Buckets of Money." The defendant objected to the administrative law judge (ALJ) assigned to hear the case on the ground that he had not been properly appointed. It was undisputed that the SEC is a "Head of Department" within the meaning of Art. II and thus eligible to be given the power of appointment, but the SEC commissioners did not choose the ALJ. Rather, they delegated that task to the staff. Hence, if the ALJ were found an "Officer of the United States," he had not been properly appointed and could not hear the case.

The D.C. Circuit upheld the SEC proceeding, then affirmed by an equally divided vote on rehearing en banc, but the Supreme Court reversed. Speaking through Justice Kagan, the Court found that the defining characteristics of an officer were that the individual (1) "occupy a 'continuing' position established by law" and (2) exercise "significant authority" under the laws of the United States. Applying these criteria and in close reliance on the earlier decision in Freytag v. Commissioner, 501 U.S. 868 (1991), the Court found that the ALJ was an officer and had to be appointed by the SEC itself rather than by its staff.

The concurrences and dissenting opinions revealed a wide range of disagreement. Justice Thomas, joined by Justice Gorsuch, concurred to suggest that "officer" should have a far broader definition than the Court approved.

Relying chiefly on history, they argued that the Framers likely understood "Officers of the United States" to encompass "all federal civil officials who perform an ongoing, statutory duty—no matter how important or significant that duty." This formula would significantly expand the class of federal employees subject to the requirements of Art. II.

Justice Sotomayor, joined by Justice Ginsburg, dissented to propose a much narrower definition. They argued that the question should turn on whether the individual in question had "the ability to make final, binding decisions on behalf of the Government." This definition would have excluded the ALJ, because he had the power only to make an "initial decision," which would then be reviewed or at least allowed by the SEC.

Justice Breyer concurred in part and dissented in part (in which part he was joined by Justices Ginsburg and Sotomayor). Breyer based his concurrence on the Administrative Procedure Act and avoided the constitutional question altogether. He was motivated to do so by a fear that declaring ALJs "Officers of the United States" would imperil provisions protecting them from removal without cause. He derived this implication from the Court's decision in Free Enterprise Fund v. Public Company Accounting Oversight Board, 561 U.S. 477 (2010), which disapproved a scheme that provided two levels of insulation between the President and an executive officer. The *Free Enterprise Fund* Court's rejection of "multilevel protection from removal" was somewhat Delphic, and it is unclear what, if any, application it might have to other executive officers. The *Lucia* majority did not address the issue.

Page 619, add at the end of Note 6:

For an argument that dismissals of cases from the federal courts on justiciability grounds should be viewed as "invitations to legislators to consider other pathways for adjudication," such as state courts, administrative agencies, and other non-Article III tribunals, see Zachary D. Clopton, Justiciability, Federalism, and the Administrative State, 103 Cornell L. Rev. 1431 (2018). For a challenge to the idea that the parties' consent should provide a constitutional basis for non-Article III adjudication, see F. Andrew Hessick, Consenting to Adjudication Outside the Article III Courts, 71 Vand. L. Rev. 715 (2018).

CHAPTER V

SUBJECT MATTER JURISDICTION

SECTION 2. DIVERSITY JURISDICTION

Page 732, add a footnote at the end of the first paragraph of Note 5:

^h In Home Depot U.S.A., Inc. v. Jackson, ___ U.S. ___, 139 S.Ct. 1743 (2019), the Court narrowly interpreted the removal provision in CAFA to preclude removal by a third-party counterclaim defendant. Citibank had filed a debt-collection action against Jackson in a North Carolina state court. Jackson then filed a counterclaim against Citibank and a third-party class action claim against Home Depot and another defendant. Citibank ultimately dismissed its claim against Jackson, after which Home Depot sought to remove the case to federal court under 28 U.S.C. §§ 1441(a) and 1453. The Court held that § 1441(a) "does not permit removal based on counterclaims at all" and that in § 1453 "Congress intended only to alter certain restrictions on removal, not expand the class of persons who can remove a class action."

The lineup was unusual. Justice Thomas wrote for a Court that was divided five to four. Justice Alito wrote the dissent, joined by Chief Justice Roberts and Justices Gorsuch and Kavanaugh.

SECTION 3. THE SUBSTANCE/PROCEDURE PROBLEM

Page 757, add after the first full paragraph:

A. Benjamin Spencer, Substance, Procedure, and the Rules Enabling Act, 66 U.C.L.A. L. Rev. 654 (2019), concludes that "the Court's failure to provide a rigorous articulation of the contours of the [Rules Enabling Act] has . . . enabled some rules to escape being detected as ultra vires judicial regulation." In particular, Spencer argues that Rules 15(c)(1) (relation back of amendments), 4(k) (relating to personal jurisdiction), and 4(n) (relating to jurisdiction over property) are problematic under a proper interpretation of the Enabling Act. As to Rule 15(c)(1), Spencer concludes:

> Given that a statute of limitations period confers on defendants a substantive right "to be free of stale claims," a Federal Rule that extinguishes that right for a person who was not sued on the same facts within the statutorily-prescribed period abridges that defendant's substantive rights. . . . The claimant's rights are enlarged by reviving an extinguished claim or by giving the claim a longer life than the state has prescribed; the defendant's rights are abridged by subjecting him to liability from which he would otherwise be protected. The transgression of the [Enabling Act] mandates, it would seem, could not be more clear.

As to Rule 4, he concludes that "Procedural rules must be confined to addressing the manner in which adjudication occurs. Jurisdictional rules address a court's power to entertain a matter at all. Congress—not the courts—has the authority to delineate the jurisdictional reach of the inferior federal courts."

SECTION 4. FINALITY AND APPELLATE REVIEW

SUBSECTION B. CIRCUIT COURT REVIEW OF DISTRICT COURT DECISIONS

Page 800, add at the end of footnote c:

Rule 42(a)(2) provides that "[i]f actions before the court involve a common question of law or fact, the court may . . . consolidate the actions . . . ." *Gelboim* left open the question whether cases consolidated under Rule 42(a) were immediately appealable when one of them was disposed of by final order.

In a unanimous opinion by Chief Justice Roberts in Hall v. Hall, 584 U.S. ___, 138 S.Ct. 1118 (2018), the Court held that such a case was immediately appealable:

> The history against which Rule 42(a) was adopted resolves any ambiguity regarding the meaning of "consolidate" in subsection (a)(2). It makes clear that one of multiple cases consolidated under the Rule retains its independent character, at least to the extent it is appealable when finally resolved, regardless of any ongoing proceedings in the other cases. . . . [C]onstituent cases retain their separate identities at least to the extent that a final decision in one is immediately appealable by the losing party.

For consideration of *Hall* in the broader context of finality in general, see Bryan Lammon, Finality, Appealability, and the Scope of Interlocutory Review, 93 Wash. L. Rev. 1809 (2018). For a more focused view on *Hall* itself, see Bryan Lammon, *Hall v. Hall*: A Lose-Lose Case for Appellate Jurisdiction, 68 Emory L.J. Online 1001 (2018).

Page 806, add after the first full paragraph:

For more recent treatment of the finality question, see Bryan Lammon, Finality, Appealability, and the Scope of Interlocutory Review, 93 Wash. L. Rev. 1809 (2018). Lammon concludes that the federal courts have interpreted the term final decision in three contexts to create three kinds of rules: (1) rules about when district court proceedings have ended and parties can take the traditional, end-of-proceedings appeal on the merits; (2) rules about when litigants can appeal before the end of those proceedings; and (3) rules limiting or expanding the scope of review in those appeals. Though related, these contexts are distinct and involve unique issues and interests. The future of federal appellate jurisdiction—whether it comes from rulemaking or further judicial decisions—must reckon with these three distinct kinds of rules and the unique interests that they entail. And successful reform must fill each of the roles that interpretations of the term "final decision" have played.

CHAPTER VI

ABSTENTION

SECTION 1. INTRODUCTION

Page 809, add a footnote at the end of the carryover paragraph at the top of the page:

^d What about criminal cases that proceed separately in state and federal court based on the same facts? Res judicata principles would not preclude multiple prosecutions because the two cases would involve different prosecuting authorities, neither of which could be bound by the actions of the other.

The Court faced this issue in Gamble v. United States, 587 U.S. ___, 139 S.Ct. 1960 (2019). Gamble pleaded guilty to a violation of an Alabama law punishing felons who possess a firearm. He was sentenced to 10 years imprisonment, all but one year of which was suspended. He then was indicted for the same instance of possession that also violated a federal criminal law. He was convicted in federal court, and sentenced to almost three more years of imprisonment. In an opinion written by Justice Alito, the Court followed "170 years of precedent" and upheld the federal conviction based on the "dual sovereignty" doctrine, under which each sovereign is permitted to pursue violations of its own laws. The Double Jeopardy Clause, the Court said, "protects individuals from being twice put in jeopardy 'for the same *offence*, not the same *conduct* or *actions*." The original understanding, the Court continued, was that "an 'offence' is defined by a law, and each law is defined by a sovereign. So where there are two sovereigns, there are two laws, and two 'offences.'" The vote was seven to two. Justices Ginsburg and Gorsuch wrote separate dissents.

Dual prosecutions based on the same facts are rare. Typically, prosecutorial agreements result in one sovereign deferring to the other. After *Gamble*, one question to be asked is when a second prosecution would be justified following an acquittal or a conviction in the other forum.

SECTION 2. *YOUNGER* ABSTENTION

Page 827, add at the end of Note 6:

See also Fred O. Smith, Jr., Abstention in the Time of Ferguson, 131 Harv. L. Rev. 2283 (2018), which argues for a *Younger* exception in cases where there "are structural or systemic constitutional flaws built into a state's procedural apparatus."

SECTION 6. INTERNATIONAL COMITY ABSTENTION

Page 906, add at the end of Note 8:

For a critique of judicial reliance on a general doctrine of international comity abstention and an argument that courts should "identify instead distinct bases for abstention in transnational cases—much as they have in domestic cases—that can then be distinctly analyzed," see Maggie Gardner, Abstention at the Border, 105 Va. L. Rev. 63, 69 (2019).

CHAPTER VII

HABEAS CORPUS

SECTION 2. REVIEW OF STATE COURT DECISIONS ON THE MERITS: AEDPA

Page 980, add to the list of other literature on AEDPA in Note 4:

LeRoy Pernell, Racial Justice and Federal Habeas Corpus as Postconviction Relief from State Convictions, 69 Mercer L. Rev. 453 (2018);

Page 986, add at the end of footnote b:

Daniel Epps, Harmless Errors and Substantial Rights, 131 Harv. L. Rev. 2117 (2018), points out that "all prior attempts to understand harmless error have proceeded from the premise that it involves a remedies question: what should a court do about a violation of the defendant's constitutional rights?" Epps argues instead that

> harmless error is inexorably tied up in the process of defining and enforcing constitutional *rights*. When asking whether an error is harmless, an appellate court should not think of itself as asking whether a particular violation of the defendant's rights is serious enough to demand the remedy of reversal. Instead, it is really asking whether a defendant's constitutional rights have been violated at all.

He concludes that this "rights-based approach" has at least one important practical payoff:

> [I]t would require courts to be clearer about the values at stake when adjudicating claims of harmless error. No longer could a court declare a broad scope of a constitutional right while in the same breath undercutting that right's effective value through the use of harmless error analysis. That would be a step forward, even if only a small one.

Page 989, add a new Note after Note 3:

3A. DECISIONS ON THE MERITS WITHOUT OPINION

Both state and federal appellate courts frequently make decisions on the merits without elaborating the reasons for their decision. Usually they are summary affirmances of a lower court decision, and usually the lower court will have given reasons for its decision. Is it fair to assume that the appellate court adopted the lower court's reasoning when it affirmed the decision?

The answer to this question when a federal court makes a summary affirmance is "no," as reflected in the following passage from Justice Gorsuch's dissent in Wilson v. Sellers, 584 U.S. ___, 138 S.Ct. 1188 (2018):

> Appellate courts usually have an independent duty to review the facts and law in the cases that come to them. Often they see errors in lower court opinions. But often, too, they may affirm on alternative bases either argued by the parties or (sometimes) apparent to them on the face of the record. See, e.g., SEC v. Chenery Corp., 318 U.S. 80, 88 (1943) (noting "the settled rule that, in reviewing the decision of a lower court, it must be affirmed if the result is correct 'although the lower court relied upon a wrong ground or gave a wrong reason'"). And a busy appellate court sometimes may not see the profit in devoting its limited resources to explaining the error and the alternative basis for affirming when the outcome is sure to

remain the same, so it issues a summary affirmance instead. To reflect these realities, this Court has traditionally warned readers *against* presuming our summary affirmance orders rest on reasons articulated in lower court opinions. Comptroller of Treasury of Md. v. Wynne, 575 U.S. ___, 135 S.Ct. 1787, 1801 (2015) (" '[A] summary affirmance is an affirmance of the judgment only,' and 'the rationale of the affirmance may not be gleaned solely from the opinion below' "). The courts of appeals have issued similar warnings for similar reasons about their own summary orders.

Typically, the reason for seeking to determine the rationale for a summary affirmance by the Supreme Court or a federal Circuit Court will be to learn whether it should have precedential effect. Is the situation different when federal courts are confronted in habeas cases with state court summary affirmances? The answer is "yes," it is different. A federal habeas court will be interested in the rationale of a state court summary disposition for an entirely different reason.

AEDPA permits federal courts to grant habeas only where a relevant state court decision "was contrary to, or involved an unreasonable application of, clearly established Federal law." In order to determine whether a state supreme court summary affirmance was "unreasonable" in its application of federal law, a federal habeas court would be obligated, one would assume, to discover how the state courts applied the applicable federal law. How should it do so when the state's highest court has said nothing?

(i) *Federal Claim Rejected Because of Procedural Foreclosure: Ylst v. Nunnemaker*

One possible rationale for the state court disposition in such a situation is an adequate and independent state ground resulting in a procedural foreclosure. Such a decision by a state court then would not involve a controlling determination of federal law in the first place.

In Ylst v. Nunnemaker, 501 U.S. 797 (1991), a federal habeas petitioner's constitutional claim had been rejected on direct appeal from his conviction because he had not raised it at trial. "[A]n objection based upon a *Miranda* violation cannot be raised for the first time on appeal," the court said. He later sought collateral review in several state courts, all of which summarily denied relief without opinion. The question before the Supreme Court was how lower federal habeas courts should understand the reasoning of the state habeas courts in such circumstances. Justice Scalia's opinion for the Court said:

> The problem we face arises, of course, because many formulary orders are not meant to convey *anything* as to the reason for the decision. Attributing a reason is therefore both difficult and artificial. We think that the attribution necessary for federal habeas purposes can be facilitated, and sound results more often assured, by applying the following presumption: Where there has been one reasoned state judgment rejecting a federal claim, later unexplained orders upholding that judgment or rejecting the same claim rest

upon the same ground. If an earlier opinion "fairly appear[s] to rest primarily upon federal law," we will presume that no procedural default has been invoked by a subsequent unexplained order that leaves the judgment or its consequences in place. Similarly where, as here, the last reasoned opinion on the claim explicitly imposes a procedural default, we will presume that a later decision rejecting the claim did not silently disregard that bar and consider the merits.

(ii) Federal Claim Rejected on the Merits: Wilson v. Sellers

In Wilson v. Sellers, 584 U.S. ___, 138 S.Ct. 1188 (2018), the last reasoned state court opinion rejected a federal claim on the merits. The ultimate question before federal habeas courts was whether a summary affirmance of that decision by a state appellate court "unreasonably" applied federal law. A preliminary question was whether the state appellate court should be taken to have relied on the same reasoning that was reflected in the lower state court disposition. The Supreme Court addressed only this preliminary question, leaving the ultimate issue for Circuit Court determination on remand.

Wilson was sentenced to death following a conviction for murder. He claimed in a state habeas proceeding that his counsel was ineffective. This claim was rejected on the ground that his counsel was not deficient and that, in any event, the alleged error (failure to offer mitigating evidence at sentencing) was not prejudicial because the evidence was "inadmissible on evidentiary grounds." The state Supreme Court summarily affirmed without explanation. In an opinion by Justice Breyer, the Court said:

> What then is the federal habeas court to do? We hold that the federal court should "look through" the unexplained decision to the last related state-court decision that does provide a relevant rationale. It should then presume that the unexplained decision adopted the same reasoning. But the State may rebut the presumption by showing that the unexplained affirmance relied or most likely did rely on different grounds than the lower state court's decision, such as alternative grounds for affirmance that were briefed or argued to the state supreme court or obvious in the record it reviewed.

The Court elaborated:

> The State points out that there could be many cases in which a "look through" presumption does not accurately identify the grounds for the higher court's decision. And we agree. We also agree that it is more likely that a state supreme court's single word "affirm" rests upon alternative grounds where the lower state court decision is unreasonable than, e.g., where the lower court rested on a state-law procedural ground, as in *Ylst*. But that is why we have set forth a presumption and not an absolute rule. And the unreasonableness of the lower court's decision itself provides some evidence that makes it less likely the state supreme court adopted the

> same reasoning. Thus, additional evidence that might not be sufficient to rebut the presumption in a case like *Ylst* would allow a federal court to conclude that counsel has rebutted the presumption in a case like this one. For instance, a federal habeas court may conclude that counsel has rebutted the presumption on the basis of convincing alternative arguments for affirmance made to the State's highest court or equivalent evidence presented in its briefing to the federal court similarly establishing that the State's highest court relied on a different ground than the lower state court, such as the existence of a valid ground for affirmance that is obvious from the state-court record. . . . A presumption that can be rebutted by evidence of, for instance, an alternative ground that was argued or that is clear in the record was the likely basis for the decision is in accord with full and proper respect for state courts. . . .

The Court then remanded the case to the Circuit Court to follow this approach in determining whether the state appellate court was "unreasonable" in its application of federal law.

Joined by Justices Thomas and Alito, Justice Gorsuch dissented. He began:

> After a state supreme court issues a summary order sustaining a criminal conviction, should a federal habeas court reviewing that decision presume it rests only on the reasons found in a lower state court opinion? The answer is no. The statute governing federal habeas review permits no such "look through" presumption. Nor do traditional principles of appellate review. In fact, we demand the *opposite* presumption for our work—telling readers that we independently review each case and that our summary affirmances may be read only as signaling agreement with a lower court's judgment and not necessarily its reasons. Because I can discern no good reason to treat the work of our state court colleagues with less respect than we demand for our own, I would reject [the Court's] presumption and must respectfully dissent.

Gorsuch reasoned:

> As the text [of AEDPA] and our precedent make clear, a federal habeas court must focus its review on the final state court decision on the merits, not any preceding decision by an inferior state court. Nor does it matter whether the final state court decision comes with a full opinion or in a summary order: the same deference is due all final state court decisions. Harrington v. Richter, 562 U.S. 86, 98 (2011).
>
> The upshot of these directions is clear. Even when the final state court decision "is unaccompanied by an explanation, the habeas petitioner's burden still must be met by showing *there was no reasonable basis* for the state court to deny relief." *Richter*, 562 U.S. at 98 (emphasis added). And before a federal court can disregard a final summary state court decision, it "must determine what

arguments or theories . . . *could have supporte[d]* the state court's decision; and then it must ask whether it is possible fair-minded jurists could disagree that those arguments or theories are inconsistent with the holding in a prior decision of this Court." Id. at 102 (emphasis added). Far from suggesting federal courts should presume a state supreme court summary order rests on views expressed in a lower court's opinion, then, AEDPA and our precedents require more nearly the *opposite* presumption: federal courts must presume the order rests on any reasonable basis the law and facts allow.

If this standard seems hard for a habeas petitioner to overcome, "that is because it was meant to be." Ibid. In AEDPA, Congress rejected the notion that federal habeas review should be "a substitute for ordinary error correction." Id. at 102–03.

There is, Gorsuch added, "some good news" in the Court's approach. The Court's elaboration of the force of its presumption "reveals just how futile this whole business really is":

[I]f, as the Court . . . tells us, a federal habeas court can always deny relief on a basis that is apparent from the record or on the basis of alternative arguments presented by the parties in state or federal proceedings, then the "look through" presumption truly means nothing and we are back where we started. . . . [A]federal habeas court is neither obliged to *look through* exclusively to the reasons given by a lower state court, nor required to *presume* that a summary order adopts those reasons.

All this is welcome news of a sort. The Court may promise us a future of foraging through presumptions and rebuttals. But at least at the end of it we rest knowing that what was true before remains true today: a federal habeas court should look at all the arguments presented in state and federal court and examine the state court record. And a federal habeas court should sustain a state court summary decision denying relief if those materials reveal a basis to do so reasonably consistent with this Court's holdings. Exactly what a federal court applying the statute and *Richter* has had to do all along. . . .

(iii) Questions and Comments

What is the debate in *Wilson* all about? At the end of the day, is there a significant difference between the majority and the dissent? Both opinions permit the denial of habeas relief if the state can show a plausible basis in federal law to justify the state court disposition, whatever the state court's reasoning may have been in fact. And both illustrate how hard it will be for a federal habeas petitioner to overcome a state court summary denial of relief. Might the message be, indeed, that appellate state courts will be better off if they say nothing?

Section 3. Procedural Limitations

Subsection A. Procedural Foreclosure

Page 1008, add at the end of the third full paragraph:

As explained in Eve Brensike Primus, Federal Review of State Criminal Convictions: A Structural Approach to Adequacy Doctrine, 116 Mich. L. Rev. 75, 83 (2017), "[c]ause and prejudice asks whether an individual defendant had a legitimate excuse for failing to comply with state procedures." The adequacy prong of the adequate and independent state ground doctrine "asks not whether the defendant should be forgiven for failing to comply with legitimate rules but whether the state's rules are legitimate in the first place—whether they warrant the respect and deference that justify procedural default."[b]

[b] Primus argues for a broader adequacy inquiry in addition to the one the Court is accustomed to making: "what is needed is a structural approach to adequacy, one that would consider how the interaction of multiple procedural rules unfairly burdens federal rights." She concludes:

> Rather than looking in each case only at the particular procedural rule that the petitioner is said to have violated, the federal courts should consider how that one rule is situated in the overall state procedural system and ask a larger question: Is the state system structured in such a way that this litigant will not have, in practice, a real opportunity to raise a federal constitutional claim? Unless the federal court is willing to look at the labyrinth, there is little chance that petitioners will ever find their way through it.

Section 4. Claims of Innocence

Page 1050, add at the end of Note 4:

Finally, for discussion of the treatment of claims of *legal* innocence, i.e., convictions or sentences under an unconstitutional or inapplicable statute, in which the author notes that the Supreme Court's reception in recent years to such claims "is noteworthy because it runs against the general trend of judges narrowing the scope of federal habeas review," see Leah M. Litman, Legal Innocence and Federal Habeas, 104 Va. L. Rev. 417, 420 (2018).

Section 5. Intersecting Issues

Subsection A. Applicability of *Teague* in State Courts

Page 1051, add a footnote after the third sentence in the second paragraph of Note 1:

[a] Lee Kovarsky, Structural Change in State Postconviction Review, 93 Notre Dame L. Rev. 443 (2017), considers the increased importance of state post-conviction review caused by the juxtaposition of expanding constitutional rights that, for one reason or another, cannot be resolved at trial and the declining availability of federal habeas relief: "In economic phrasing, demand for collateral process is rising at the same time that federal supply is falling." Among other things, Kovarsky discusses the next main case, *Montgomery v. Louisiana*, at length.

Page 1054, add at the end of footnote e:

See also Ruthanne M. Deutsch, Federalizing Retroactivity Rules: The Unrealized Promise of *Danforth v. Minnesota* and the Unmet Obligation of State Courts to Vindicate Federal Constitutional Rights, 44 Fla. St. U. L. Rev. 53 (2016).

CHAPTER VIII

STATE SOVEREIGN IMMUNITY AND THE ELEVENTH AMENDMENT

SECTION 1. NATURE OF THE LIMITATION

Page 1100, add a new Note after Note 5:

5A. PROPER TERMINOLOGY

The sovereign immunity of the states in federal courts has often been referred to as "Eleventh Amendment immunity." This term has frequently been used by the Supreme Court,[h] and it is sometimes used in the Notes in this Chapter. It reflects the fact that the Eleventh Amendment is the only part of the Constitution that directly limits suits against states in a federal court. But ever since *Hans*, it has been clear that the Supreme Court's conception of state sovereign immunity is broader than the terms of the Eleventh Amendment.

The Court now conceives of the Eleventh Amendment as merely clarifying that, contrary to *Chisholm v. Georgia*, the Constitution's grant of Article III power to hear disputes between out-of-state citizens and states did not displace state sovereign immunity. The source of immunity, under this view, is not the Eleventh Amendment, but rather the constitutional structure as informed by the sovereign rights that the states would have had at the time the Constitution was adopted.

The Court explained this point in Alden v. Maine, 527 U.S. 706, 713 (1999):

> We have . . . sometimes referred to the States' immunity from suit as "Eleventh Amendment immunity." The phrase is convenient shorthand but something of a misnomer, for the sovereign immunity of the States neither derives from, nor is limited by, the terms of the Eleventh Amendment. Rather, as the Constitution's structure, its history, and the authoritative interpretations by this Court make clear, the States' immunity from suit is a fundamental aspect of the sovereignty which the States enjoyed before the ratification of the Constitution, and which they retain today (either literally or by virtue of their admission into the Union upon an equal footing with the other States) except as altered by the plan of the Convention or certain constitutional Amendments.

---

[h] See, for example, Seminole Tribe of Florida v. Florida, 517, U.S. 44, 58, 59 (1996). *Seminole Tribe* is a main case in Section 2 of this Chapter.

As a result, the term that probably best accords with the Court's current approach to this topic is simply "state sovereign immunity." This is the language that the Court used, for example, in its most recent decision in this area, *Franchise Tax Board v. Hyatt*, which is excerpted as a main case below.

Page 1125, add a new Note after Note 3:

3A. FEDERAL INJUNCTIONS TO ENFORCE STATE LAW: *PENNHURST STATE SCHOOL AND HOSPITAL V. HALDERMAN*

The Pennhurst State School and Hospital was a Pennsylvania institution for the care of the mentally retarded. A class action was brought in federal court on behalf of residents of Pennhurst against the Hospital, some of its officials, the state Department of Public Welfare, and a number of other defendants to enforce rights alleged to arise from the federal Constitution, from federal legislation, and from state legislation. After long and complex litigation, the Circuit Court approved an injunction requiring comprehensive changes in living conditions at the Hospital on the basis of rights found to have been created by the *state* legislation.

In Pennhurst State School and Hospital v. Halderman, 465 U.S. 89 (1984), the Supreme Court held the injunction forbidden by the Eleventh Amendment:

> We first address the contention that respondents' state law claim is not barred by the Eleventh Amendment because it seeks only prospective relief as defined in *Edelman v. Jordan*. The Court of Appeals held that if the judgment below rested on federal law, it could be entered against petitioner state officials under the doctrine established in *Edelman* and *Ex parte Young* even though the prospective financial burden was substantial and on-going. The court assumed, and respondents assert, that this reasoning applies as well when the official acts in violation of state law. This argument misconstrues the basis of the doctrine established in *Young* and *Edelman*.
>
> [T]he injunction in *Ex parte Young* was justified, notwithstanding the obvious impact on the state itself, on the view that sovereign immunity does not apply because an official who acts unconstitutionally is "stripped of his official or representative character." . . . Our decisions repeatedly have emphasized that the *Young* doctrine rests on the need to promote the vindication of federal rights.
>
> The Court also has recognized, however, that the need to promote the supremacy of federal law must be accommodated to the constitutional immunity of the states. This is the significance of *Edelman v. Jordan*. We recognized that the prospective relief authorized by *Young* "has permitted the Civil War amendments to the Constitution to serve as a sword, rather than merely a shield, for those whom they were designed to protect." But we declined to extend the fiction of *Young* to encompass retroactive relief, for to do so would effectively eliminate the constitutional immunity of the

states.... In sum *Edelman*'s distinction between prospective and retroactive relief fulfills the underlying purpose of *Ex parte Young* while at the same time preserving to an important degree the constitutional immunity of the states.

The need to reconcile competing interests is wholly absent, however, when a plaintiff alleges that a state official has violated *state* law. In such a case the entire basis for the doctrine of *Young* and *Edelman* disappears. A federal court's grant of relief against state officials on the basis of state law, whether prospective or retroactive, does not vindicate the supreme authority of federal law. On the contrary, it is difficult to think of a greater intrusion on state sovereignty than when a federal court instructs state officials on how to conform their conduct to state law. Such a result conflicts directly with the principles of federalism that underlie the Eleventh Amendment. We conclude that *Young* and *Edelman* are inapplicable in a suit against state officials on the basis of state law.

Justice Stevens, joined by Justices Brennan, Marshall, and Blackmun, dissented.

A footnote in Justice Powell's *Pennhurst* opinion states that "[a]t the time the suit was filed, suits against Pennsylvania were permitted only where expressly authorized by the legislature," and further that Pennsylvania later enacted a statute on sovereign immunity, "including an express preservation of its immunity from suit in federal court." The dissent made no mention of this point, but as David Shapiro points out in Comment, Wrong Turns: The Eleventh Amendment and the *Pennhurst* Case, 98 Harv. L. Rev. 61, 76–78 (1984), the story is more complicated than at first appears.

The *Pennhurst* litigation began in 1974. At that time, Pennsylvania's sovereign immunity was apparently intact. In 1978, however, the state Supreme Court abrogated the doctrine retroactively. The legislature overturned that decision, but the Pennsylvania Supreme Court held that the statute could not bar litigation of a cause of action that had already accrued at the time of its passage. Thus, it is at least arguable that, under the decisions of the Pennsylvania Supreme Court (and contrary to the wishes of the legislature), there was no state doctrine of sovereign immunity applicable to the *Pennhurst* litigation.

Should state law have mattered? *Erie* would seem to require that federal courts use state law to decide questions of state sovereign immunity from state law claims. Martha Field takes exactly that position. See Martha Field, The Eleventh Amendment and Other Sovereign Immunity Doctrines: Congressional Imposition of Suit upon the States, 126 U. Pa. L. Rev. 1203, 1254 n.240 (1978). Does it follow that if state law permits an action against the state, the federal courts should be free to entertain it? In Atascadero State Hospital v. Scanlon, 473 U.S. 234, 241 (1985), the Court said:

> The test for determining whether a state has waived its immunity from federal-court jurisdiction is a stringent one. Although a state's general waiver of sovereign immunity may subject it to suit in state court, it is not enough to waive the immunity

guaranteed by the Eleventh Amendment. As we explained just last term, "a state's constitutional interest in immunity encompasses not merely *whether* it may be sued, but *where* it may be sued." Pennhurst State School and Hospital v. Halderman, 465 U.S. 89, 99 (1984). Thus, in order for a state statute or constitutional provision to constitute a waiver of Eleventh Amendment immunity, it must specify the state's intention to subject itself to suit in *federal court*.

Does it follow from *Atascadero* that *Pennhurst* was right?

Page 1129, replace the Notes on the Intersection of the Eleventh Amendment and State Law, pages 1129–33, with a new Main Case and Notes:

Franchise Tax Board v. Hyatt
Supreme Court of the United States, 2019.
587 U.S. ___, 139 S.Ct. 1485.

■ JUSTICE THOMAS delivered the opinion of the Court.

This case, now before us for the third time, requires us to decide whether the Constitution permits a State to be sued by a private party without its consent in the courts of a different State. We hold that it does not and overrule our decision to the contrary in Nevada v. Hall, 440 U.S. 410 (1979).

I

In the early 1990s, respondent Gilbert Hyatt earned substantial income from a technology patent for a computer formed on a single integrated circuit chip. Although Hyatt's claim was later canceled, his royalties in the interim totaled millions of dollars. Prior to receiving the patent, Hyatt had been a long-time resident of California. But in 1991, Hyatt sold his house in California and rented an apartment, registered to vote, obtained insurance, opened a bank account, and acquired a driver's license in Nevada. When he filed his 1991 and 1992 tax returns, he claimed Nevada—which collects no personal income tax, as his primary place of residence.

Petitioner Franchise Tax Board of California (Board), the state agency responsible for assessing personal income tax, suspected that Hyatt's move was a sham. Thus, in 1993, the Board launched an audit to determine whether Hyatt underpaid his 1991 and 1992 state income taxes by misrepresenting his residency. In the course of the audit, employees of the Board traveled to Nevada to conduct interviews with Hyatt's estranged family members and shared his personal information with business contacts. In total, the Board sent more than 100 letters and demands for information to third parties. The Board ultimately concluded that Hyatt had not moved to Nevada until April 1992 and owed California more than $10 million in back taxes, interest, and penalties. Hyatt protested the audit before the Board, which upheld the audit after an 11-year administrative proceeding. The appeal of that decision remains pending before the California Office of Tax Appeals.

In 1998, Hyatt sued the Board in Nevada state court for torts he alleged the agency committed during the audit. After the trial court denied in part the Board's motion for summary judgment, the Board petitioned the Nevada Supreme Court for a writ of mandamus ordering dismissal on the ground that the State of California was immune from suit. The Board argued that, under the Full Faith and Credit Clause, Nevada courts must apply California's statute immunizing the Board from liability for all injuries caused by its tax collection. The Nevada Supreme Court rejected that argument and held that, under general principles of comity, the Board was entitled to the same immunity that Nevada law afforded Nevada agencies—that is, immunity for negligent but not intentional torts. We granted certiorari and unanimously affirmed, holding that the Full Faith and Credit Clause did not prohibit Nevada from applying its own immunity law to the case. Franchise Tax Bd. of Cal. v. Hyatt, 538 U.S. 488, 498–99 (2003) (*Hyatt I*). Because the Board did not ask us to overrule *Nevada v. Hall*, we did not revisit that decision.

On remand, the trial court conducted a 4-month jury trial that culminated in a verdict for Hyatt that, with prejudgment interest and costs, exceeded $490 million. On appeal, the Nevada Supreme Court rejected most of the damages awarded by the lower court, upholding only a $1 million judgment on one of Hyatt's claims and remanding for a new damages trial on another. Although the court recognized that tort liability for Nevada state agencies was capped at $50,000 under state law, it nonetheless held that Nevada public policy precluded it from applying that limitation to the California agency in this case. We again granted certiorari and this time reversed, holding that the Full Faith and Credit Clause required Nevada courts to grant the Board the same immunity that Nevada agencies enjoy. Franchise Tax Bd. of Cal. v. Hyatt, 578 U.S. ___, ___–___, 136 S.Ct. 1277, 1281–83 (2016) (*Hyatt II*). Although the question was briefed and argued, the Court was equally divided on whether to overrule *Hall* and thus affirmed the jurisdiction of the Nevada Supreme Court. On remand, the Nevada Supreme Court instructed the trial court to enter damages in accordance with the statutory cap for Nevada agencies.

We granted, for a third time, the Board's petition for certiorari. The sole question presented is whether *Nevada v. Hall* should be overruled.[1]

II

Nevada v. *Hall* is contrary to our constitutional design and the understanding of sovereign immunity shared by the States that ratified the Constitution. Stare decisis does not compel continued adherence to this

---

[1] Hyatt argues that the law-of-the-case doctrine precludes our review of this question, but he failed to raise that nonjurisdictional issue in his brief in opposition. We therefore deem this argument waived. . . .

erroneous precedent. We therefore overrule *Hall* and hold that States retain their sovereign immunity from private suits brought in the courts of other States.

A

Hall held that the Constitution does not bar private suits against a State in the courts of another State. The opinion conceded that States were immune from such actions at the time of the founding, but it nonetheless concluded that nothing "implicit in the Constitution" requires States "to adhere to the sovereign-immunity doctrine as it prevailed when the Constitution was adopted." 440 U.S. at 417–18, 424–27. Instead, the Court concluded that the Founders assumed that "prevailing notions of comity would provide adequate protection against the unlikely prospect of an attempt by the courts of one State to assert jurisdiction over another." Id. at 419. The Court's view rested primarily on the idea that the States maintained sovereign immunity vis-à-vis each other in the same way that foreign nations do, meaning that immunity is available only if the forum State "voluntar[ily]" decides "to respect the dignity of the [defendant State] as a matter of comity." Id. at 416.

The *Hall* majority was unpersuaded that the Constitution implicitly altered the relationship between the States. In the Court's view, the ratification debates, the Eleventh Amendment, and our sovereign-immunity precedents did not bear on the question because they "concerned questions of federal-court jurisdiction." Id. at 420. The Court also found unpersuasive the fact that the Constitution delineates several limitations on States' authority, such as Article I powers granted exclusively to Congress and Article IV requirements imposed on States. Despite acknowledging "that ours is not a union of 50 wholly independent sovereigns," *Hall* inferred from the lack of an express sovereign immunity granted to the States and from the Tenth Amendment that the States retained the power in their own courts to deny immunity to other States.

Chief Justice Burger, Justice Blackmun, and Justice Rehnquist dissented.

B

Hall's determination that the Constitution does not contemplate sovereign immunity for each State in a sister State's courts misreads the historical record and misapprehends the "implicit ordering of relationships within the federal system necessary to make the Constitution a workable governing charter and to give each provision within that document the full effect intended by the Framers." Id. at 433 (Rehnquist, J., dissenting). As Chief Justice Marshall explained, the Founders did not state every postulate on which they formed our Republic—"we must never forget, that it is *a constitution* we are expounding." McCulloch v. Maryland, 17 U.S. (4 Wheat.) 316, 407 (1819). And although the Constitution assumes that the States retain their sovereign immunity except as otherwise provided, it also fundamentally adjusts the States' relationship with each other and curtails their ability, as sovereigns, to decline to recognize each other's immunity.

1

After independence, the States considered themselves fully sovereign nations. As the Colonies proclaimed in 1776, they were "Free and Independent States" with "full Power to levy War, conclude Peace, contract Alliances, establish Commerce, and to do all other Acts and Things which Independent States may of right do." Declaration of Independence ¶ 4. Under international law, then, independence "entitled" the Colonies "to all the rights and powers of sovereign states." McIlvaine v. Coxe's Lessee, 8 U.S. (4 Cranch) 209, 212 (1808).

"An integral component" of the States' sovereignty was "their immunity from private suits." Federal Maritime Comm'n v. South Carolina Ports Authority, 535 U.S. 743, 751–52 (2002); see Alden v. Maine, 527 U.S. 706, 713 (1999) ("[A]s the Constitution's structure, its history, and the authoritative interpretations by this Court make clear, the States' immunity from suit is a fundamental aspect of the sovereignty which the States enjoyed before the ratification of the Constitution, and which they retain today . . ."). This fundamental aspect of the States' "inviolable sovereignty" was well established and widely accepted at the founding. . . .

The Founders believed that both "common law sovereign immunity" and "law-of-nations sovereign immunity" prevented States from being amenable to process in any court without their consent. See James E. Pfander, Rethinking the Supreme Court's Original Jurisdiction in State-Party Cases, 82 Cal. L. Rev. 555, 581–88 (1994); see also Caleb Nelson, Sovereign Immunity as a Doctrine of Personal Jurisdiction, 115 Harv. L. Rev. 1559, 1574–79 (2002). The common-law rule was that "no suit or action can be brought against the king, even in civil matters, because no court can have jurisdiction over him." 1 W. Blackstone, Commentaries on the Laws of England 235 (1765) (Blackstone). The law-of-nations rule followed from the "perfect equality and absolute independence of sovereigns" under that body of international law. Schooner Exchange v. McFaddon, 11 U.S. (7 Cranch) 116, 137 (1812). . . .

The founding generation thus took as given that States could not be haled involuntarily before each other's courts. See Ann Woolhandler, Interstate Sovereign Immunity, 2006 S.Ct. Rev. 249, 254–59. . . .

In short, at the time of the founding, it was well settled that States were immune under both the common law and the law of nations. The Constitution's use of the term "States" reflects both of these kinds of traditional immunity. And the States retained these aspects of sovereignty, "except as altered by the plan of the Convention or certain constitutional Amendments." *Alden*, 527 U.S. at 713.

2

One constitutional provision that abrogated certain aspects of this traditional immunity was Article III, which provided a neutral federal forum in which the States agreed to be amenable to suits brought by other States. Art. III, § 2; see *Alden*, 527 U.S. at 755. . . .

The States, in ratifying the Constitution, similarly surrendered a portion of their immunity by consenting to suits brought against them by the United States in federal courts. See Principality of Monaco v. Mississippi, 292 U. S. 313, 328 (1934). "While that jurisdiction is not conferred by the Constitution in express words, it is inherent in the constitutional plan." *Monaco*, 292 U.S. at 329. . . .

The Antifederalists worried that Article III went even further by extending the federal judicial power over controversies "between a State and Citizens of another State." They suggested that this provision implicitly waived the States' sovereign immunity against *private* suits in federal courts. But "[t]he leading advocates of the Constitution assured the people in no uncertain terms" that this reading was incorrect. *Alden*, 527 U.S. at 716. According to Madison:

> "[A federal court's] jurisdiction in controversies between a state and citizens of another state is much objected to, and perhaps without reason. It is not in the power of individuals to call any state into court. The only operation it can have, is that, if a state should wish to bring a suit against a citizen, it must be brought before the federal court. This will give satisfaction to individuals, as it will prevent citizens, on whom a state may have a claim, being dissatisfied with the state courts." Elliot's Debates 533. . . .

Not long after the founding, however, the Antifederalists' fears were realized. In Chisholm v. Georgia, 2 U.S. (2 Dall.) 419 (1793), the Court held that Article III allowed the very suits that the "Madison-Marshall-Hamilton triumvirate" insisted it did not. *Hall*, 440 U.S. at 437 (Rehnquist, J., dissenting). That decision precipitated an immediate "furor" and "uproar" across the country. Congress and the States accordingly acted swiftly to remedy the Court's blunder by drafting and ratifying the Eleventh Amendment.

The Eleventh Amendment confirmed that the Constitution was not meant to "rais[e] up" any suits against the States that were "anomalous and unheard of when the Constitution was adopted." Hans v. Louisiana, 134 U.S. 1, 18 (1890). Although the terms of that Amendment address only "the specific provisions of the Constitution that had raised concerns during the ratification debates and formed the basis of the *Chisholm* decision," the "natural inference" from its speedy adoption is that "the Constitution was understood, in light of its history and structure, to preserve the States' traditional immunity from private suits." *Alden*, at 723–24. . . .

Consistent with this understanding of state sovereign immunity, this Court has held that the Constitution bars suits against nonconsenting States in a wide range of cases. See, e.g., *Federal Maritime Comm'n*, supra (actions by private parties before federal administrative agencies); *Alden*, supra (suits by private parties against a State in its own courts); Blatchford v. Native Village of Noatak, 501 U.S. 775 (1991) (suits by Indian tribes in federal court); *Monaco*, supra (suits by foreign states in federal court); Ex parte New York, 256 U.S. 490 (1921) (admiralty suits by private parties in federal court); Smith v. Reeves, 178 U.S. 436 (1900) (suits by federal corporations in federal court).

3

Despite this historical evidence that interstate sovereign immunity is preserved in the constitutional design, Hyatt insists that such immunity exists only as a "matter of comity" and can be disregarded by the forum State. He reasons that, before the Constitution was ratified, the States had the power of fully independent nations to deny immunity to fellow sovereigns; thus, the States must retain that power today with respect to each other because "nothing in the Constitution or formation of the Union altered that balance among the still-sovereign states." Brief for Respondent 14. . . .

The problem with Hyatt's argument is that the Constitution affirmatively altered the relationships between the States, so that they no longer relate to each other solely as foreign sovereigns. Each State's equal dignity and sovereignty under the Constitution implies certain constitutional "limitation[s] on the sovereignty of all of its sister States." World-Wide Volkswagen Corp. v. Woodson, 444 U.S. 286, 293 (1980). One such limitation is the inability of one State to hale another into its courts without the latter's consent. The Constitution does not merely allow States to afford each other immunity as a matter of comity; it embeds interstate sovereign immunity within the constitutional design. Numerous provisions reflect this reality.

To begin, Article I divests the States of the traditional diplomatic and military tools that foreign sovereigns possess. Specifically, the States can no longer prevent or remedy departures from customary international law because the Constitution deprives them of the independent power to lay imposts or duties on imports and exports, to enter into treaties or compacts, and to wage war. Compare Art. I, § 10, with Declaration of Independence ¶ 4 (asserting the power to "levy War, conclude Peace, contract Alliances, [and] establish Commerce").

Article IV also imposes duties on the States not required by international law. The Court's Full Faith and Credit Clause precedents, for example, demand that state-court judgments be accorded full effect in other States and preclude States from "adopt[ing] any policy of hostility to the public Acts" of other States. *Hyatt II*, 578 U.S. at ___, 136 S.Ct. at 1281; see Art. IV, § 1. States must also afford citizens of each State "all Privileges and Immunities of Citizens in the several States" and honor extradition requests upon "Demand of the executive Authority of the State" from which the fugitive fled. Art. IV, § 2. Foreign sovereigns cannot demand these kinds of reciprocal responsibilities absent consent or compact. . . .

The Constitution also reflects implicit alterations to the States' relationships with each other, confirming that they are no longer fully independent nations. For example, States may not supply rules of decision governing "disputes implicating the[ir] conflicting rights." Texas Industries, Inc. v. Radcliff Materials, Inc., 451 U.S. 630, 641 (1981). Thus, no State can apply its own law to interstate disputes over borders, Cissna v. Tennessee, 246 U.S. 289, 295 (1918), water rights, Hinderlider v. La Plata River & Cherry Creek Ditch Co., 304 U.S. 92, 110 (1938), or the interpretation of interstate compacts, Petty v. Tennessee-Missouri Bridge Comm'n, 359 U.S. 275, 278–79 (1959). The States would have had the raw power to apply their own law to such matters before they entered the Union, but the Constitution implicitly forbids that exercise of power because the "interstate . . . nature of the controversy makes it inappropriate for state law to control." *Texas Industries*, supra, at 641. Some subjects that were decided by pure "political power" before ratification now turn on federal "rules of law." Rhode Island v. Massachusetts, 37 U.S. (12 Pet.) 657, 737 (1838). See Bradford R. Clark, Federal Common Law: A Structural Reinterpretation, 144 U. Pa. L. Rev. 1245, 1322–31 (1996).

Interstate sovereign immunity is similarly integral to the structure of the Constitution. Like a dispute over borders or water rights, a State's assertion of compulsory judicial process over another State involves a direct conflict between sovereigns. The Constitution implicitly strips States of any power they once had to refuse each other sovereign immunity, just as it denies them the power to resolve border disputes by political means. Interstate immunity, in other words, is "implied as an essential component of federalism." *Hall*, 440 U.S. at 430–31 (Blackmun, J., dissenting).

Hyatt argues that we should find no right to sovereign immunity in another State's courts because no constitutional provision explicitly grants that immunity. But this is precisely the type of "ahistorical literalism" that we have rejected when "interpreting the scope of the States' sovereign immunity since the discredited decision in *Chisholm*." *Alden*, 527 U.S. at 730; see id. at 736 ("[T]he bare text of the Amendment is not an exhaustive description of the States' constitutional immunity from suit"). In light of our constitutional structure, the historical understanding of state immunity, and the swift enactment of the Eleventh Amendment after the Court departed from this understanding in *Chisholm*, "[i]t is not rational to suppose that the sovereign power should be dragged before a court." Elliot's Debates 555 (Marshall). Indeed, the spirited historical debate over Article III courts and the immediate reaction to *Chisholm* make little sense if the Eleventh Amendment were the only source of sovereign immunity and private suits against the States could already be brought in "partial, local tribunals." Elliot's Debates 532 (Madison). Nor would the Founders have objected so strenuously to a neutral federal forum for private suits against States if they were open to a State being sued in a different State's courts. Hyatt's view thus inverts the Founders' concerns about state-court parochialism. *Hall*, supra, at 439 (Rehnquist, J., dissenting).

Moreover, Hyatt's ahistorical literalism proves too much. There are many other constitutional doctrines that are not spelled out in the Constitution but are nevertheless implicit in its structure and supported by historical practice—including, for example, judicial review, Marbury v. Madison, 5 U.S. (1 Cranch) 137, 176–80 (1803); intergovernmental tax immunity, *McCulloch*, 17 U.S. (4 Wheat.) at 435–36; executive privilege, United States v. Nixon, 418 U.S. 683, 705–06 (1974); executive immunity, Nixon v. Fitzgerald, 457 U.S. 731, 755–58 (1982); and the President's removal power, Myers v. United States, 272 U.S. 52, 163–64 (1926). Like these doctrines, the States' sovereign immunity is a historically rooted principle embedded in the text and structure of the Constitution.

C

With the historical record and precedent against him, Hyatt defends *Hall* on the basis of stare decisis. But stare decisis is " 'not an inexorable command,' " Pearson v. Callahan, 555 U.S. 223, 233 (2009), and we have held that it is "at its weakest when we interpret the Constitution because our interpretation can be altered only by constitutional amendment," Agostini v. Felton, 521 U.S. 203, 235 (1997). The Court's precedents identify a number of factors to consider, four of which warrant mention here: the quality of the decision's reasoning; its consistency with related decisions; legal developments since the decision; and reliance on the decision.

The first three factors support our decision to overrule *Hall*. We have already explained that *Hall* failed to account for the historical understanding of state sovereign immunity and that it failed to consider how the deprivation of traditional diplomatic tools reordered the States' relationships with one another. We have also demonstrated that *Hall* stands as an outlier in our sovereign-immunity jurisprudence, particularly when compared to more recent decisions.

As to the fourth factor, we acknowledge that some plaintiffs, such as Hyatt, have relied on *Hall* by suing sovereign States. Because of our decision to overrule *Hall*, Hyatt unfortunately will suffer the loss of two decades of litigation expenses and a final judgment against the Board for its egregious conduct. But in virtually every case that overrules a controlling precedent, the party relying on that precedent will incur the loss of litigation expenses and a favorable decision below. Those case-specific costs are not among the reliance interests that would persuade us to adhere to an incorrect resolution of an important constitutional question.

* * *

Nevada v. *Hall* is irreconcilable with our constitutional structure and with the historical evidence showing a widespread preratification understanding that States retained immunity from private suits, both in their own courts and in other courts. We therefore overrule that decision.

Because the Board is thus immune from Hyatt's suit in Nevada's courts, the judgment of the Nevada Supreme Court is reversed, and the case is remanded for proceedings not inconsistent with this opinion.

It is so ordered.

■ JUSTICE BREYER, with whom JUSTICE GINSBURG, JUSTICE SOTOMAYOR, and JUSTICE KAGAN join, dissenting.

Can a private citizen sue one State in the courts of another? Normally the answer to this question is no, because the State where the suit is brought will choose to grant its sister States immunity. But the question here is whether the Federal Constitution *requires* each State to grant its sister States immunity, or whether the Constitution instead *permits* a State to grant or deny its sister States immunity as it chooses.

We answered that question 40 years ago in Nevada v. Hall, 440 U.S. 410 (1979). The Court in *Hall* held that the Constitution took the permissive approach, leaving it up to each State to decide whether to grant or deny its sister States sovereign immunity. Today, the majority takes the contrary approach—the absolute approach—and overrules *Hall*. I can find no good reason to overrule *Hall*, however, and I consequently dissent.

I

Hall involved a suit brought by a California resident against the State of Nevada in the California courts. We rejected the claim that the Constitution entitled Nevada to absolute immunity. We first considered the immunity that States possessed as independent sovereigns before the Constitution was ratified. And we then asked whether ratification of the Constitution altered the principles of state sovereign immunity in any relevant respect. At both steps, we concluded, the relevant history and precedent refuted the claim that States are entitled to absolute immunity in each other's courts.

A

Hall first considered the immunity that States possessed before ratification. "States considered themselves fully sovereign nations" during this period, and the Court in *Hall* therefore asked whether sovereign nations would have enjoyed absolute immunity in each other's courts at the time of our founding.

The answer was no. At the time of the founding, nations granted other nations sovereign immunity in their courts not as a matter of legal obligation but as a matter of choice, i.e., of comity or grace or consent. Foreign sovereign immunity was a doctrine "of implied consent by the territorial sovereign . . . deriving from standards of public morality, fair dealing, reciprocal self-interest, and respect." National City Bank of N.Y. v. Republic of China, 348 U.S. 356, 362 (1955). Since customary international law made the matter one of choice, a nation could withdraw that sovereign immunity if it so chose. . . .

... Drawing on the comparison to foreign nations, the Court in *Hall* emphasized that California had made a sovereign decision not to "exten[d] immunity to Nevada as a matter of comity." 440 U.S. at 418. Unless some constitutional rule required California to grant immunity that it had chosen to withhold, the Court "ha[d] no power to disturb the judgment of the California courts." Id.

B

The Court in *Hall* next held that ratification of the Constitution did not alter principles of state sovereign immunity in any relevant respect. The Court concluded that express provisions of the Constitution—such as the Eleventh Amendment and the Full Faith and Credit Clause of Article IV—did not require States to accord each other sovereign immunity. And the Court held that nothing "implicit in the Constitution" treats States differently in respect to immunity than international law treats sovereign nations. Id. at 418.

To the contrary, the Court in *Hall* observed that an express provision of the Constitution undermined the assertion that States were absolutely immune in each other's courts. Unlike suits brought against a State in the State's own courts, *Hall* noted, a suit against a State in the courts of a different State "necessarily implicates the power and authority of" both States. Id. at 416. The defendant State has a sovereign interest in immunity from suit, while the forum State has a sovereign interest in defining the jurisdiction of its own courts. The Court in *Hall* therefore justified its decision in part by reference to "the Tenth Amendment's reminder that powers not delegated to the Federal Government nor prohibited to the States are reserved to the States or to the people." Id. at 425. Compelling States to grant immunity to their sister States would risk interfering with sovereign rights that the Tenth Amendment leaves to the States. . . .

II

The majority disputes both *Hall*'s historical conclusion regarding state immunity before ratification and its conclusion that the Constitution did not alter that immunity. But I do not find the majority's arguments convincing.

A

The majority asserts that before ratification "it was well settled that States were immune under both the common law and the law of nations." The majority thus maintains that States were exempt from suit in each other's courts.

But the question in *Hall* concerned the *basis* for that exemption. Did one sovereign have an absolute right to an exemption from the jurisdiction of the courts of another, or was that exemption a customary matter, a matter of consent that a sovereign might withdraw? As to that question, nothing in the majority's opinion casts doubt on *Hall*'s conclusion that

States—like foreign nations—were accorded immunity as a matter of consent rather than absolute right. . . .

B

The majority next argues that "the Constitution affirmatively altered the relationships between the States" by giving them immunity that they did not possess when they were fully independent. The majority thus maintains that, whatever the nature of state immunity before ratification, the Constitution accorded States an absolute immunity that they did not previously possess.

The most obvious problem with this argument is that no provision of the Constitution gives States absolute immunity in each other's courts. The majority does not attempt to situate its newfound constitutional immunity in any provision of the Constitution itself. Instead, the majority maintains that a State's immunity in other States' courts is "implicit" in the Constitution, "embed[ded] . . . within the constitutional design," and reflected in " 'the plan of the Convention.' " . . .

. . . I can find nothing in the "plan of the Convention" or elsewhere to suggest that the Constitution converted what had been the customary practice of extending immunity by consent into an absolute federal requirement that no State could withdraw. None of the majority's arguments indicates that the Constitution accomplished any such transformation.

The majority argues that the Constitution sought to preserve States' "equal dignity and sovereignty." That is true, but tells us nothing useful here. When a citizen brings suit against one State in the courts of another, both States have strong sovereignty-based interests. In contrast to a State's power to assert sovereign immunity in its own courts, sovereignty interests here lie on both sides of the constitutional equation. . . .

[W]here the Constitution alters the authority of States vis-à-vis other States, it tends to do so explicitly. The Import-Export Clause cited by the majority, for example, creates "harmony among the States" by preventing them from "burden[ing] commerce . . . among themselves." Michelin Tire Corp. v. Wages, 423 U.S. 276, 283, 285 (1976). The Full Faith and Credit Clause, also invoked by the majority, prohibits States from adopting a "policy of hostility to the public Acts" of another State. Franchise Tax Bd. of Cal. v. Hyatt, 578 U.S. ___, ___, 136 S.Ct. 1277, 1281 (2016). By contrast, the Constitution says nothing explicit about interstate sovereign immunity. . . .

III

In any event, stare decisis requires us to follow *Hall*, not overrule it. See Planned Parenthood of Southeastern Pa. v. Casey, 505 U.S. 833, 854–55 (1992); see also Kimble v. Marvel Entertainment, LLC, 576 U.S. ___, ___–___, 135 S.Ct. 2401, 2409 (2015). Overruling a case always requires " 'special justification.' " *Kimble*, 576 U.S. at ___, 135 S.Ct. at 2409. What could that justification be in this case? The majority does not find one.

The majority believes that *Hall* was wrongly decided. But "an argument that we got something wrong—even a good argument to that effect—cannot by itself justify scrapping settled precedent." *Kimble*, 576 U.S. at ___, 135 S.Ct. at 2409. Three dissenters in *Hall* also believed that *Hall* was wrong, but they recognized that the Court's opinion was "plausible." 440 U.S. at 427 (opinion of Blackmun, J.). While reasonable jurists might disagree about whether *Hall* was correct, that very fact—that *Hall* is not obviously wrong—shows that today's majority is obviously wrong to overrule it. . . .

The dissenters in *Hall* feared its "practical implications." 440 U.S. at 443 (opinion of Rehnquist, J.). But I can find nothing in the intervening 40 years to suggest that this fear was well founded. The Board and its amici have, by my count, identified only 14 cases in 40 years in which one State has entertained a private citizen's suit against another State in its courts. See Brief for Petitioner 46–47; Brief for State of Indiana et al. as Amici Curiae 13–14. In at least one of those 14 cases, moreover, the state court eventually agreed to dismiss the suit against its sister State as a matter of comity. How can it be that these cases, decided over a period of four decades, show *Hall* to be unworkable?

The *Hall* issue so rarely arises because most States, like most sovereign nations, are reluctant to deny a sister State the immunity that they would prefer to enjoy reciprocally. Thus, even in the absence of constitutionally mandated immunity, States normally grant sovereign immunity voluntarily. States that fear that this practice will be insufficiently protective are free to enter into an interstate compact to guarantee that the normal practice of granting immunity will continue. . . .

Perhaps the majority believes that there has been insufficient reliance on *Hall* to justify preserving it. But any such belief would ignore an important feature of reliance. The people of this Nation rely upon stability in the law. Legal stability allows lawyers to give clients sound advice and allows ordinary citizens to plan their lives. Each time the Court overrules a case, the Court produces increased uncertainty. To overrule a sound decision like *Hall* is to encourage litigants to seek to overrule other cases; it is to make it more difficult for lawyers to refrain from challenging settled law; and it is to cause the public to become increasingly uncertain about which cases the Court will overrule and which cases are here to stay. . . .

* * *

It is one thing to overrule a case when it "def[ies] practical workability," when "related principles of law have so far developed as to have left the old rule no more than a remnant of abandoned doctrine," or when "facts have so changed, or come to be seen so differently, as to have robbed the old rule of significant application or justification." *Casey*, 505 U.S. at 854–55. It is far more dangerous to overrule a decision only because five Members of a later Court come to agree with earlier dissenters on a difficult legal question. The majority has surrendered to the temptation to overrule *Hall* even though it is a well-reasoned decision that has caused no serious practical problems in the four decades since we decided it. Today's decision can only cause one to wonder which cases the Court will overrule next. I respectfully dissent.

NOTES ON FRANCHISE TAX BOARD V. HYATT

1. NEVADA V. HALL

California residents were injured when their car was struck by a vehicle being driven on official business by an employee of the state of Nevada. The accident occurred in California. The plaintiffs sued in a California state court, naming as defendants the Nevada employee's estate (he was killed in the accident) and the state. Personal jurisdiction was acquired over the state under a California statute authorizing service of process on nonresident motorists. The California courts upheld a jury verdict against Nevada for more than $1 million, notwithstanding a Nevada statute limiting recoveries against the state to $25,000. In Nevada v. Hall, 440 U.S. 410 (1979), the Supreme Court affirmed.

In an opinion by Justice Stevens, the Court denied that California was bound by federal law to respect Nevada's sovereign immunity. The Court observed that there was nothing in either the Eleventh Amendment or in Article III that "provide[s] any basis, explicit or implicit, for this Court to impose limits on the powers of California exercised in this case." The Court also reasoned that the constitutional Founders appeared to have assumed that "prevailing notions of comity would provide adequate protection against the unlikely prospect of an attempt by the courts of one State to assert jurisdiction over another." As for broader principles of state sovereignty, the Court reasoned:

> It may be wise policy, as a matter of harmonious interstate relations, for States to accord each other immunity or to respect any established limits on liability. They are free to do so. But if a federal court were to hold, by inference from the structure of our Constitution and nothing else, that California is not free in this case to enforce its policy of full compensation, that holding would constitute the real intrusion on the sovereignty of the States—and the power of the people—in our Union.

Justice Blackmun, joined by Chief Justice Burger and by Justice Rehnquist, dissented, saying that, although the majority's decision was "plausible," he would find "a constitutional doctrine of interstate sovereign immunity" implied as an essential component of the federal system. Justice Rehnquist, joined by the Chief Justice, wrote separately, adding that the result reached by the majority "destroys the framers' careful allocation of responsibility among the state and federal judiciaries, and makes nonsense of the effort embodied in the Eleventh Amendment to preserve the doctrine of sovereign immunity."

For criticism of *Nevada v. Hall*, see Ann Woolhandler, Interstate Sovereign Immunity, 2006 Sup. Ct. Rev. 249. For a defense of *Hall*, see William Baude, Sovereign Immunity and the Constitutional Text, 103 Va. L. Rev. 1 (2017). For discussion of the case in the broader context of choice of law generally, see Patrick J. Borchers, Is the Supreme Court Really Going to Regulate Choice of Law Involving States?, 50 Creighton L. Rev. 7 (2016).

2. *ALDEN V. MAINE*

The Supreme Court's conception of state sovereign immunity has evolved significantly since *Nevada v. Hall*. This is especially evident in decisions addressing Congress's authority to abrogate immunity, which are addressed in Section 2 of this chapter. A noteworthy example is Alden v. Maine, 527 U.S. 706 (1999), a five-four decision in which the Court held that Congress lacked authority under Article I of the Constitution to abrogate a state's immunity in the state's own courts. This was true, reasoned the Court, even though the Eleventh Amendment does not apply to state courts. The Court explained:

> [The Court's] holdings reflect a settled doctrinal understanding, consistent with the views of the leading advocates of the Constitution's ratification, that sovereign immunity derives not from the Eleventh Amendment but from the structure of the original Constitution itself. . . . The Eleventh Amendment confirmed rather than established sovereign immunity as a constitutional principle; it follows that the scope of the States' immunity from suit is demarcated not by the text of the Amendment alone but by fundamental postulates implicit in the constitutional design.

The Court proceeded to conclude, based on "history, practice, precedent, and the structure of the Constitution," that "the States retain immunity from private suit in their own courts, an immunity beyond the congressional power to abrogate by Article I legislation." The Court distinguished *Nevada v. Hall* as follows:

> Our opinion in *Hall* did distinguish a State's immunity from suit in federal court from its immunity in the courts of other States; it did not, however, address or consider any differences between a State's sovereign immunity in federal court and in its own courts. Our reluctance to find an implied constitutional limit on the power of the States cannot be construed, furthermore, to support an analogous reluctance to find implied constitutional limits on the power of the Federal Government. The Constitution, after all, treats the powers of the States differently from the powers of the Federal Government. . . .
>
> Our decision in *Hall* thus does not support the argument urged by petitioners here. The decision addressed neither Congress' power to subject States to private suits nor the States' immunity from suit in their own courts. In fact, the distinction drawn between a sovereign's immunity in its own courts and its immunity in the courts of another sovereign, as well as the reasoning on which this

distinction was based, are consistent with, and even support, the proposition urged by the respondent here—that the Constitution reserves to the States a constitutional immunity from private suits in their own courts which cannot be abrogated by Congress.

3. QUESTIONS AND COMMENTS ON *FRANCHISE TAX BOARD V. HYATT*

According to the Court in *Franchise Tax*, what is the source of the states' sovereign immunity? To what extent, if at all, is the text of the Eleventh Amendment relevant to this immunity? The Court contends that the Constitution treated the relationship between U.S. states differently than the way that international law at that time treated the relationship between sovereign nations. How, according to the Court, is this historical point relevant to the immunity issue in this case? What is the dissent's response? Both the majority and dissent invoke considerations relating to state sovereignty: the majority invokes a sovereign right of a state not to be haled into a sister state court without its consent, and the dissent invokes a sovereign right of a state to open its courts up to suits against other states. What is the majority's rationale for favoring the first sovereignty interest over the second?

In overturning *Nevada v. Hall*, what justifications does the Court give for departing from stare decisis? Is it simply that a new Court majority has concluded that *Hall* was wrongly decided, as the dissent contends? The Court notes, among other things, that "*Hall* stands as an outlier in our sovereign-immunity jurisprudence, particularly when compared to more recent decisions." If the reasoning of a decision is inconsistent with the reasoning of subsequent decisions, should stare decisis still apply? Does overturning a decision in order to make the case law more coherent undermine legal stability, as suggested by the dissent?

SECTION 2. CONSENT AND CONGRESSIONAL ABROGATION

Page 1177, add to footnote b:

Graham K. Bryant, The Historical Argument for State Sovereign Immunity in Bankruptcy Proceedings, 87 Miss. L.J. 49 (2018).

CHAPTER IX
42 U.S.C. § 1983

SECTION 2. OFFICIAL IMMUNITIES

Page 1274, add a footnote at the end of Note 10:

ᶠ For a rare analysis of qualified immunity that differentiates between *Bivens* and § 1983, see Katherine Mims Crocker, Qualified Immunity and Constitutional Structure, 117 Mich. L. Rev. 1405 (2019). Crocker argues that the extension of qualified immunity in *Harlow* might be viewed as a "compensating adjustment" for the "judicial overreach" of creating *Bivens* in the first place. Qualified immunity in actions authorized by § 1983 would necessarily stand on different ground, perhaps influenced by considerations of federalism.

Page 1274, add a new Note after Note 10:

11. BIBLIOGRAPHY

In addition to the many articles on specific aspects of qualified immunity (see, for example, the articles on the "order-of-battle" issue in the next section), there is continuing, indeed accelerating, debate about qualified immunity in general. Prominent critics of qualified immunity include William Baude, Is Qualified Immunity Unlawful?, 106 Calif. L. Rev. 45 (2018); Alan K. Chen, The Intractability of Qualified Immunity, 93 Notre Dame L. Rev. 1937 (2018); Joanna C. Schwartz, The Case Against Qualified Immunity, 93 Notre Dame L. Rev. 1797 (2018); and Fred O. Smith, Jr., Formalism, Ferguson, and the Future of Qualified Immunity, 93 Notre Dame L. Rev. 2093 (2018).

Scott Michelman, The Branch Best Qualified to Abolish Immunity, 93 Notre Dame L. Rev. 1999 (2018), assumes that qualified immunity should be eliminated and argues that the judiciary should do so. Karen M. Blum, Qualified Immunity: Time to Change the Message, 93 Notre Dame L. Rev. 1887 (2018), argues that the Court should embrace respondeat superior for government employers and thus "fix" qualified immunity by making it irrelevant. John F. Preis, Qualified Immunity and Fault, 93 Notre Dame L. Rev. 1969 (2018), argues that qualified immunity as currently applied does not accurately assess fault and perhaps cannot do so.

A partial defense of qualified immunity appears in Aaron L. Nielson and Christopher J. Walker, A Qualified Defense of Qualified Immunity, 93 Notre Dame L. Rev. 1853 (2018). And an empirical assessment of how it works at trial appears in Alexander A. Reinert, Qualified Immunity at Trial, 93 Notre Dame L. Rev. 2065 (2018) (partly joining issue with Joanna Schwartz, supra). The application of qualified immunity in a particular context is explored in David M. Shapiro and Charles Hogle, The Horror Chamber: Unqualified Immunity in Prison, 93 Notre Dame L. Rev. 2021 (2018).

Finally, Michael L. Wells, Qualified Immunity After *Ziglar v. Abbasi*: The Case for a Categorical Approach, 68 Am. U. L. Rev. 379 (2018), proposes that qualified immunity should be scrapped as a comprehensive doctrine but retained for some specific constitutional violations based on analysis of the costs and benefits in particular contexts.